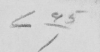

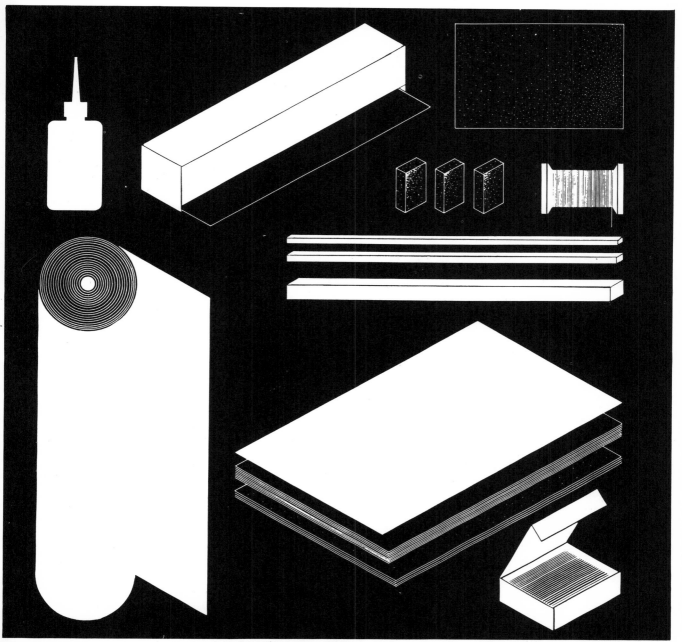

ARCHITECTURE: A book of projects for young adults

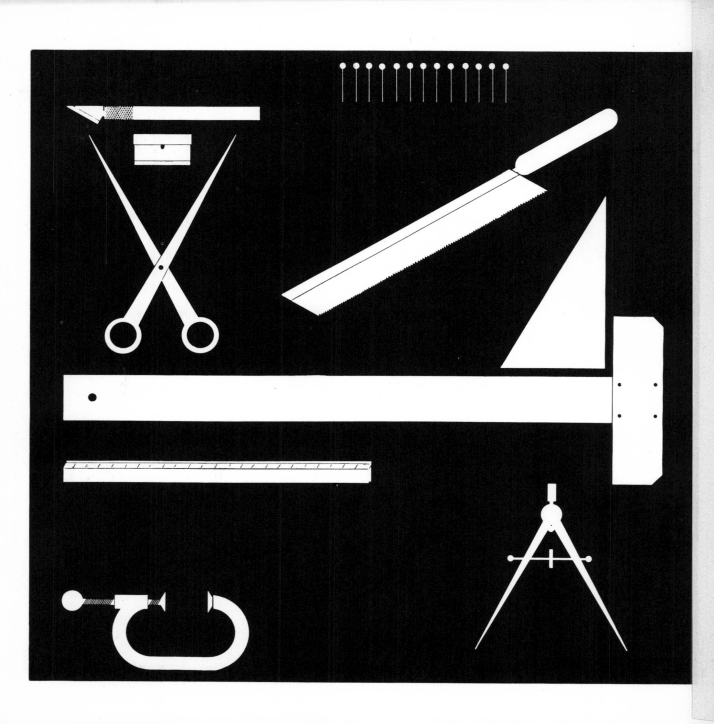

ARCHITECTURE:
A book of projects for young adults

written and illustrated by **Forrest Wilson**

REINHOLD BOOK CORPORATION   **New York**   **Amsterdam**   **London**

For

Betty, Jonathan and Robert

© 1968, Reinhold Book Corporation
All rights reserved
Printed in the United States of America
Library of Congress Catalog Card Number 67-24701

Designed by Myron Hall III
Printed by New York Lithographing Corporation
Bound by William Marley Company
Published by Reinhold Book Corporation
430 Park Avenue, New York, N.Y. 10022

CONTENTS

Thanks to
MARIA POLUSHKIN
who taught me that drawing and writing a book
are only half the battle

About the book
and its use

There are three parts to this book — old architecture, modern architecture and the language of architecture. The first two sections tell you about building, which is the architectural alphabet. The third tells about texture, scale and space which are the words of the architectural language.

You will learn both the alphabet and the language in "do it yourself" working projects. The projects require only simple, inexpensive tools and ordinary materials. Everything that is needed for each project is listed, followed by illustrated instructions for building and testing. Architectural and building terms are defined in the text with further elaboration in the illustrated glossary at the back of the book.

We believe that both learning and building can be enjoyable activities and we hope this book will prove us right.

PART 1
OLD ARCHITECTURE

Early man worked with simple materials and primitive tools to provide his basic needs of protection and shelter. The forms of the earliest buildings were dictated by three basic considerations: availability of material, the ability to work it, and that motivating force of design — man's compulsion to never let "well enough alone."

Prehistoric builders instinctively selected size and intuitively judged structural possibilities. Within these limits they created forms pleasing to themselves. This process, which we now call architectural design, has not changed appreciably throughout history. As you work on the projects in this book you will intuitively be making choices bounded by the limits of your knowledge, skill, and the materials you work with. This is the same thing that the architect has always done, from the cave to the skyscraper.

Important buildings in the period of classical or

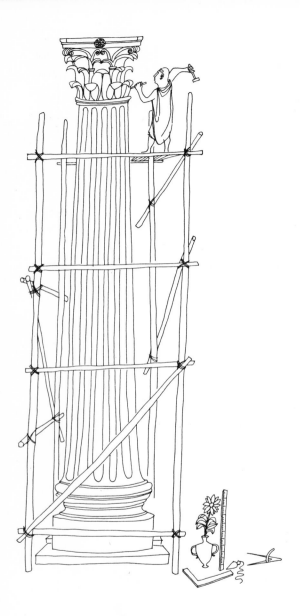

old architecture were built of brick and stone. Since the materials were strong but their bonding mortars weak, they had to be balanced against the pull of gravity so they would hold together.

In simple structures, stone lintels were short heavy and thick, and columns that supported them were closely spaced. The result was more sculpture than building because so much material was used to hold the building up, that there was hardly any interior space. The invention of arches, vaults and domes made it possible to use stone to greater advantage to create large spaces inside the building. These are forms made up of the arch curve, which is necessary to put masonry into compression. The secret of these buildings is the use of thrust and counter thrust to balance the building and withstand the force of gravity.

This principle dominated architecture from the very beginning until about one hundred years ago. Most of the old buildings that we admire were built using this idea and its variations. It is for this reason that we have devoted the first section of this book to them.

IT'S A BALANCED WORLD

Building is the creation of systems of balance. Of all the animals, man is perhaps the best qualified to understand this activity, for he spends his upright life balancing himself on his ridiculously thin ankles.

Building begins with balance. The trick is to balance movements against each other. The sum of all the forces tending to demolish the building must be countered by the sum of all the forces that stabilize it. Force and counterforce are the two halves of the equation of equilibrium which is the basic idea of architectural construction. So, let us begin with the idea of balance.

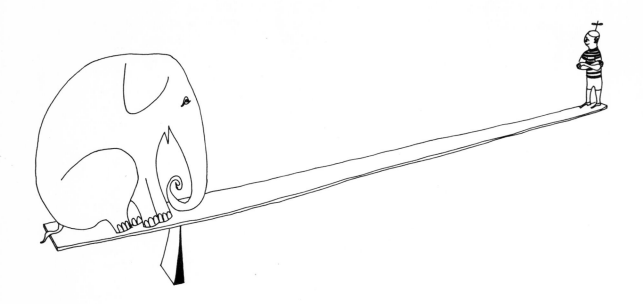

EQUAL EQUAL

Two children of different weights on a seesaw soon find that there is a simple trick to balancing each other. The heavier must sit closer to the center than the lighter. If he is twice as heavy, he must sit one half as far away from the center as does the other child. On a very strong seesaw a seventy-five pound boy could balance a modest sized, three thousand pound elephant, if the elephant sat still at one foot from the center and the boy did not fidget at forty feet from the same point. The equation is simple. The weight of the elephant, times his distance from the center must equal the weight of the boy times his distance from the same point. Three thousand times one equals seventy-five times forty ($3000 \times 1 = 75 \times 40$).

This idea can be easily illustrated by a simple experiment.

PROJECT 1 — Balancing weight and distance.

Materials; Any straight flat ruler, several sugar cubes identical in size and the edge of a desk or table to balance on.

Procedure: Balance the flat ruler on the edge of the desk or table (find an edge that is sharp, not rounded). It will balance at its center. Take two sugar cubes, place one at four inches from the center on one side of the ruler and the other at four inches from the center on the other. The ruler

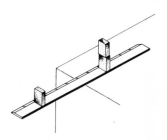

will continue to balance. Leave one cube at four inches and take two cubes and place them at two inches from the center on the opposite side of the ruler. The ruler will continue to balance because $1 \times 4 = 2 \times 2$.

You can continue to experiment with this idea, balancing various combinations of cubes and distances to equal each other. For example one cube at six inches will balance three cubes at two inches and so forth.

While the cubes balance themselves through weight and distance the ruler must counterbalance the tendency to break under the strain. An easy way to understand this principle is to place a heavy book on your head. You will feel stress and strain. The stress is the weight of the book pushing toward the earth and the strain is the weight you feel in your body as it is pressed between the book and the floor. In this instance your body is acting like a column.

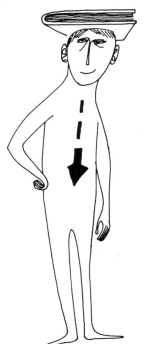

Now if you wish to feel the stresses in the ruler, hold the book at arm's length. It will feel much heavier than it did on your head. Your arm forms a cantilever like the extension on either side of the center of the ruler. Your shoulder is experiencing the strain of the weight of the book times its distance. The book has not increased in weight but the strain has been multiplied by the length of your arm.

The arrows you see on the drawing indicate the direction of the force or push. When the book is on your head the push is straight down through your body as the arrow indicates, but when it is held at arm's length the direction of the push is down and clockwise around your shoulder as the direction of that arrow shows. Throughout the book a black arrow will be used to indicate the direction of a force.

THE BALANCING BRICK

We will begin our study of the balancing act, that is architectural construction, with the humblest of all building materials, the common brick. Man created bricks out of the simplest of all natural elements — ordinary mud. He formed and dried the wet earth into bricks then piled them high into the air in massive walls. He even taught the brick to defy gravity with that most ingenious invention, the arch.

At first bricks were made by hand, later they were manufactured in wooden forms, dried in the sun, and occasionally lightly burned in ovens. Modern technology has devised machinery to make bricks faster, and make them harder by burning them at high temperatures, but the methods used in laying bricks have not changed appreciably from the time of their invention in Mesopotamia five or six thousand years before the birth of Christ. Occasionally, in architectural history, a building material is so well suited to its purpose that it cannot be improved. The brick is one of these materials.

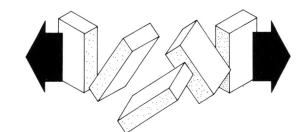

The form of the brick was dictated by necessity. It was originally designed as it is today, to be picked up by the mason in one hand while he holds his trowel in the other. This fact determines its form and its use in construction.

Bricks being small, comparatively weak units must be bonded into a strong integral mass. Since bricks are stronger than the mortar which holds them together they must be placed in a staggered sequence so as to eliminate a continuous plane of mortar.

Bricks are strong in compression (their ability to withstand being pushed against) but weak in tension (they can easily be pulled apart). Therefore, the forms of brick architecture have to be compressive so that bricks resting upon each other transmit their weight down to the earth without pulling. The trick is to interlock these comparatively weak individual units into one solid balancing mass.

You can experiment with sugar cubes to see how this works.

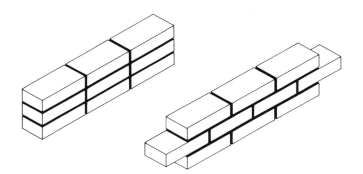

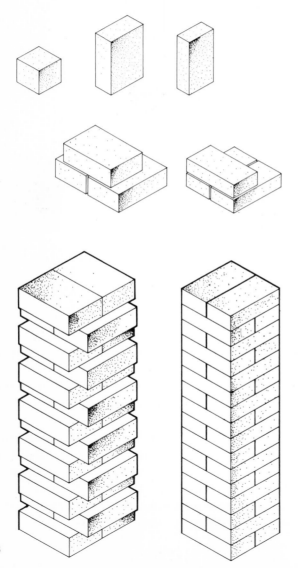

A WORD ABOUT SUGAR CUBES

The closer the size of the cube comes to the proportion of a standard brick the better it is for your purpose. Square cubes will not be of much use to you here.

The standard modular brick is nearly half as wide as it is long. When they are placed across each other the edges will come out even, with two widths equalling one length.

If your sugar cubes are not brick size, and they probably will not be, your columns will look like the first drawing instead of the second. It will work just as well even though it will not look exactly like the drawings do in the book. The cubes in the book are drawn to brick dimensions.

PROJECT 2 — A masonry column.

Materials: One box of rectangular sugar cubes, white glue such as "Elmers" and plenty of waxed paper.

Procedure: Use the waxed paper to spread on the working surface to keep the glue from sticking to it. First, build a column as high as you can by stacking the cubes singly. Note that as the column gets higher it has a greater tendency to bend and fall. Now build a column two cubes wide stacked next to each other. Does the two cube column tend to split vertically between the cubes? Third, build

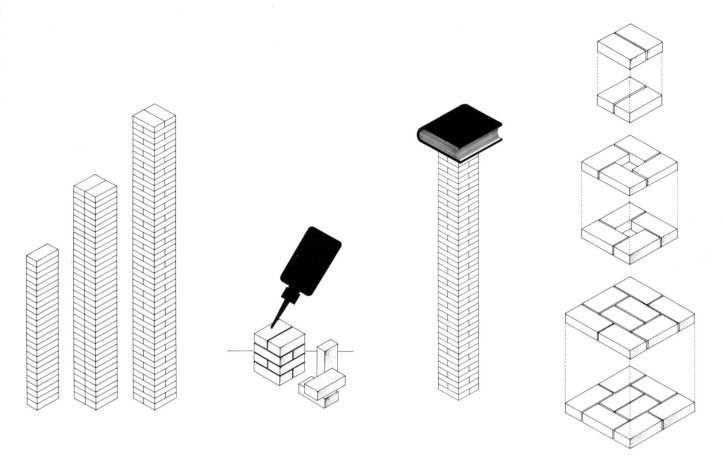

a column two cubes wide but place every other cube at right angles to the one beneath it. This is called bonding. Observe how much higher the bonded column will rise than the other two.

Dismantle the bonded column and reassemble it gluing the cubes together. Observe how much more stable the glued column is. You are using the glue as you would mortar in a real brick wall.

When you have built the glued column as high as you can, place books on top of it, one at a time, to see how many books it will hold. Continue to add books until it breaks. When it starts to fail,

watch carefully. You will see that before the column breaks it will begin to bend. If the column were thicker, say one and a half or two cubes wide, do you think it could be built higher? What is the relationship between column thickness and column height?

The masonry wall presents much the same problem as the masonry column. Its units must be bonded for strength. The thicker it is the higher it can be built. If it is supported by walls perpendicular to it, it will have more stability as you will discover in the following project.

PROJECT 3 — A masonry wall.

Materials: Two boxes of rectangular sugar cubes, white glue and waxed paper.

Procedure: Build a sugar cube wall by placing the cubes on top of each other, but instead of building them into a square make them form a flat plane. If you build two such walls about eight cubes high, parallel to each other you can test how strong they are by placing a large book across them. If they hold the first book, place more books on top until the walls fall down. Watch carefully the way the walls fall. Do they tip together, bend? What happens?

To see how walls strengthen each other you can build two walls again, but this time put one at right angles to the other to form an L. Where the walls meet, bond the bricks together as you did with the column. Now if you place books on top of the sugar cube L you will find that it will hold much more weight than the two unconnected walls. It will also be found that these walls can be built higher.

If you wish to find out how much stronger mortar will make walls you can glue the cubes together and repeat these experiments.

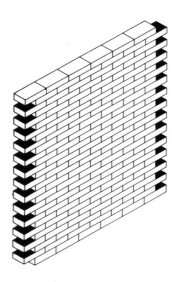

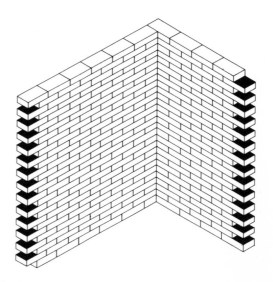

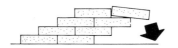

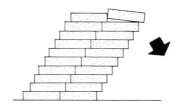

THE CORBEL

Balancing masonry in the air to span columns and walls presents a much more complicated problem than building the columns and walls themselves.

If you build a beam of bricks you know that the only thing that will keep the bricks from sliding by each other is the mortar. Such a beam will scarcely support its own weight, and that for only a short distance.

Bricks, as you remember, have very little pulling strength (tension) so they must be placed in such a way that they are subject only to pushing forces (compression).

In the corbel, the forces of compression are utilized by placing one brick above the other, each projecting slightly beyond the one beneath. In this way the bending forces in each brick are minimized.

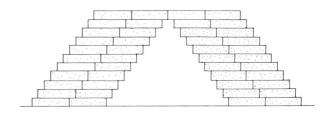

PROJECT 4 — Build a Corbel.

Materials: Box of sugar cubes.

Procedure: Place cubes on top of each other with the end cube of each course (row) projecting about one third of its length over the front edge of the cube beneath it. You will notice that unless there are enough cubes behind the projecting end cubes the construction will fall forward. You will also notice that it is possible to stack the cubes higher if the projection is shorter. There is a relationship of projection to height in a corbel the same as there was in the column.

If you construct two such corbels opposite each other, ten or eleven cubes high and about five inches apart so that the top cubes meet each other, you will have a pyramidal opening. This is how corbels are used to span openings.

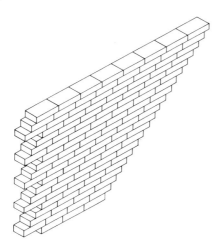

THE ARCH

The use of the arch will permit you to put your sugar cubes to work in the most economical way, that is, span the longest distance with the least number of cubes. But, the arch also presents problems. It tends, depending on its rise (height), to push sideways at its base. This is called the spring of the arch. (An arch with all of its parts named will be found in the glossary at the back of the book).

The sugar cubes used to make the arch must be supported until the last cube has been put into place. It is therefore necessary to hold the sugar cubes in place with a framework (the arch center) until it is completed. The center is then removed and the arch stands by itself.

Before you build your arch you must first build an arch center. The following project tells you how this is done.

PROJECT 5 — Build an arch center.

Materials: Any kind of cheap thin cardboard such as that found on the back of tablets of paper or used by the laundry to stiffen ironed shirts. White glue and waxed paper.

Tools: Tools for cutting such as a single edged razor blade, mat knife or scissors, straight pins.

Procedure: Mark out two half circles on the cardboard with either a compass or by drawing around the bottom of a round can. Cut them out. Mark out a strip of cardboard one inch wide and about thirteen or fourteen inches long, depending upon the diameter of your circle. Glue the strip to the round edges of the half circles as is shown in the drawing. Use pins to hold until glue dries. When this has dried you will be ready to build the arch on top of it. Remember, use the waxed paper to keep the glue from sticking to your working surface.

PROJECT 6 — Build a sugar cube arch.

Materials: Sugar cubes (about one half a box), #2 sandpaper (medium coarseness) and white glue.
Procedure: Cover the arch center you have just made with a strip of waxed paper about one and one half inches wide and fourteen or fifteen inches long. This is to prevent the sugar cubes from sticking to it. Begin placing the sugar cubes on the arch center. You can use either the long or the short edge of the cubes. Do not place them flat in this project. Since the edge of the cubes placed against the arch center will form a smaller circle than the circle formed by the outside edges, the cubes must be sanded to fit tightly against each other. Place the first cube on the table and the next one on top of it. Remove it, then sand its side and front edge to fit tightly against the other sugar cube and the arch center. When it fits, glue the two cubes together. Follow the same procedure with each cube as you build the arch around the arch center. It is best to build up from each side of the arch toward the top. When the last cube has been set, completing your arch, leave it to dry overnight. If you are working at home you could place the sugar cube arch in the oven to dry at low heat. Don't put the cardboard center or the waxed paper in the oven.

Testing: When the glue has dried, remove the center. The arch will stand by itself. Place sugar cubes on top of the arch. Note that the arch tends to spread at the bottom and break apart at the top. If you place a number of cubes at the spring of the arch you will find that you can place more weight on top. From this you can see how important thick buttresses, which the cubes at the side represent, are for arched and vaulted buildings.

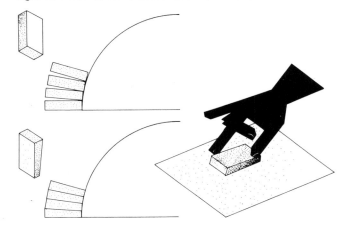

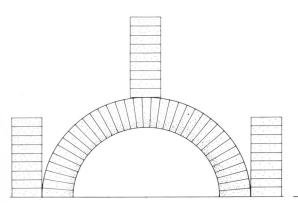

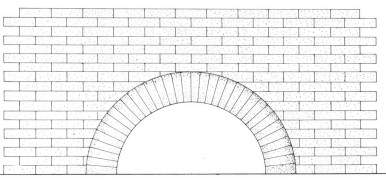

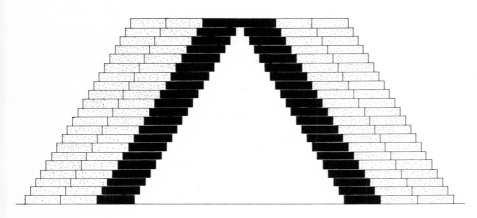

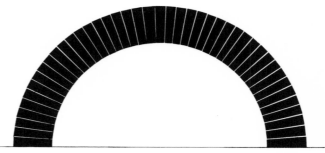

To compare the differences between corbels and arches examine the drawing. Both methods of construction span the same distance. The black cubes in relation to the white show how much more material is needed in a corbelled construction. The corbel has been built at an angle of about sixty degrees which is the most effective angle for corbels.

The three little figures represent the difference between the corbel and the arch. Corbelled arches are in reality two separate structures leaning against each other, while a true arch is one construction bridging two points.

THE CORBEL AND THE ARCH COMBINED

The principle of the corbel and the arch can be combined. As you remember, the corbel has a tendency to fall forward if not held in place by a mass of material. The arch on the other hand wants to push back in the opposite direction. These two forces can be made to balance each other in a combined construction as shown in the drawing.

The corbel pushes forward and the arch pushes back canceling each other and providing a means of spanning two walls or columns with a very attractive architectural form.

You can build a combined corbel and arch, but it will require a complicated center and lots of patience.

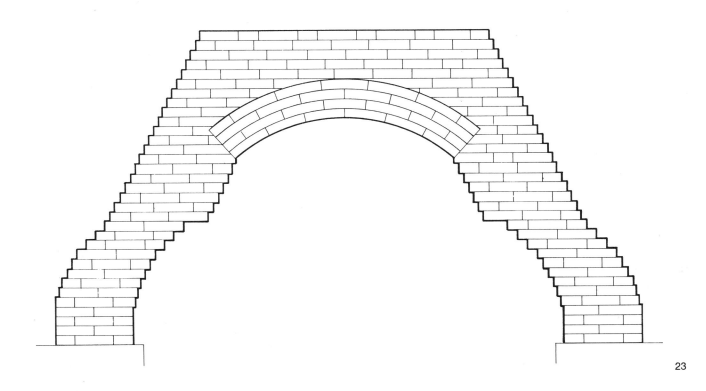

PROJECT 7 — Build a combined corbel and arch.

Materials: Two boxes of sugar cubes, cheap cardboard.

Tools: Cutting instruments, pencil, ruler and compass.

Procedure: Do not glue the cubes in this project so that you may better observe their balancing action. This is a delicate construction and you may have to try several times to accomplish your purpose.

Mark and cut out the shape of the corbel and arch on the cardboard (single thickness) as shown

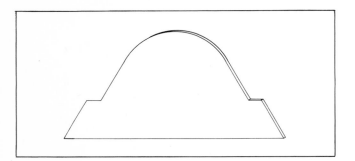

in the drawing. Build the cubes around it. Remove the cardboard very gently. If the construction begins to fall apart redesign it and try again. If the corbelled section starts to fall forward, the arch should have more side push; if the sides of the corbel push back the arch is too strong. You will have to vary the angle of the corbel against the rise of the arch.

Arches can be a variety of shapes. Designers have experimented with this beautiful form since the beginning of time. In these drawings you see a number of different forms of the arch. If you will look carefully at the center point (the round dot) and the head of the arrow you will see that these arches are drawn with a series of curves using a compass. You can build some arch centers scribing them with a compass as shown in the drawings. When sugar cube arches are built over them and tested you will find that most of them are decorative, that is, their geometry (form) does not improve their load bearing capacity.

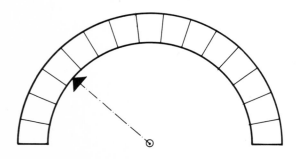

Semi-circular

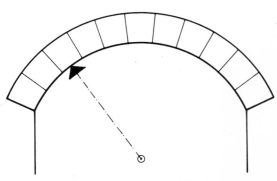

Segmental

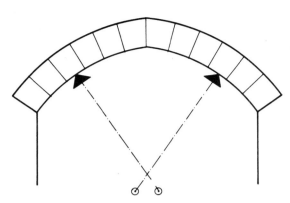

Pointed, Equilateral

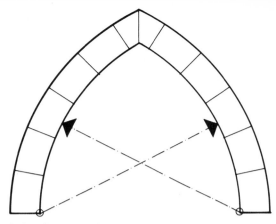

Pointed, segmental

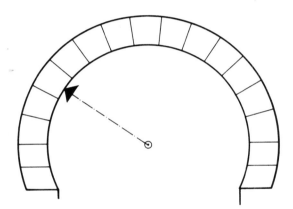

Horseshoe

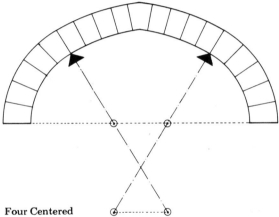

Four Centered

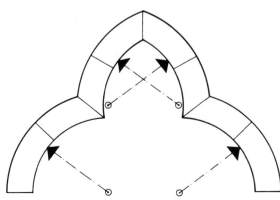

Pointed trefoil

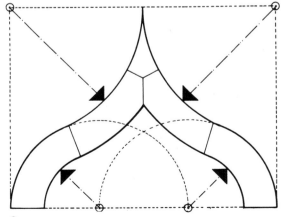

Ogee

THE IDEAL ARCH FORM

The best structural form for the arch was discovered by an ingenious thinker who realized that pushing and pulling are sometimes opposite ways of doing the same thing. He reasoned that a chain held between two points will form a natural pulling shape. Its links are free to move so they take the form that will allow them to pull against each other in the most efficient way as they themselves are pulled toward the earth by the forces of gravity. This shape is called a catenary and resembles a parabola. It is very easy to make a catenary arch.

PROJECT 8 — Build a center for a catenary arch.

Materials: A piece of light cotton string like that used to wrap packages in stores or to fly kites, about twelve or fourteen inches long, cheap light cardboard, white glue and waxed paper.
Procedure: Soak the string in white glue until it is saturated. This can be done by laying the string on the waxed paper and covering it with glue. Hold the string between your fingers, allowing it to form a regular upside down arched shape. If the shape

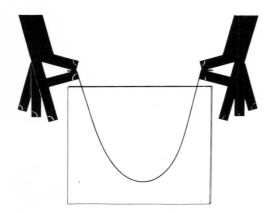

the string takes is not even, it does not have enough glue. You can control the form of the arch by moving your fingers — holding the ends closer to each other or further apart.

Very gently move the string against the cardboard so that the arc is not pushed out of shape. With the string sticking to it, lay the cardboard flat and leave to dry. This should take about one hour.

When the string has dried, cut out around it to make one-half of an arch center. To make the other, lay the cutout against another piece of cardboard and draw around it. Then cut out a thin strip of cardboard about one inch wide and long enough to be bent around the two sides of your center. Glue this in place, and you are ready to start gluing cubes around it as you did with the semicircular arches. This arch can be tested to see how strong it is. If you wish to make a comparison of the structural properties of the two arches due to their difference in shape, then make a semicircular arch of the same span as the catenary and test them both. Place an equal amount of weight upon each and increase it equally until one of the arches collapses. You will find that the catenary arch is much the stronger of the two.

THE BUTTRESS

Gothic cathedrals are famous for their pointed arches, but they had other structural principles even more remarkable. Gothic buildings are much lighter than any stone buildings preceding them, because the Gothic builders, instead of building continuous heavy stone walls counteracted the thrust of their arches at given points with buttresses. This left the intervening walls free for the beautiful stained glass windows. The famous flying buttress that looks like half an arch, was used in the middle ages as a means of reaching into the air to buttress the arch at exactly the place that it was needed.

The principle is quite simple. In some ways it resembles our previous problem of the combined corbel and the arch. As the arch thrust pushes out, the flying buttress pushes back. It is a balance of two forces working against each other.

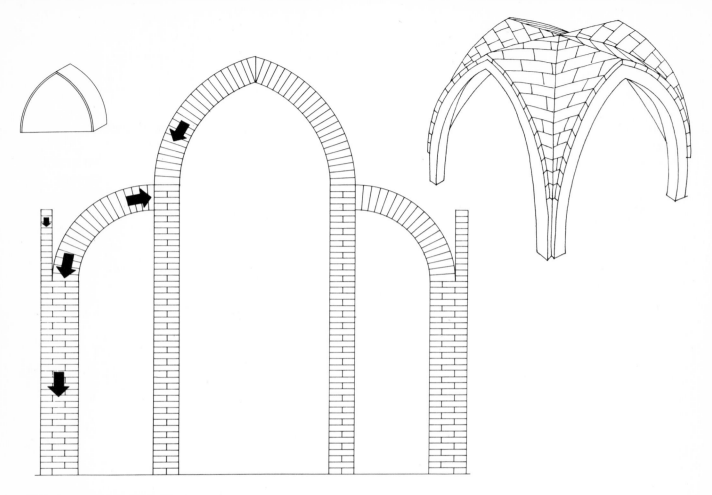

PROJECT 9 — Build a flying buttress.

Materials: Several boxes of sugar cubes, cheap light cardboard, waxed paper, sandpaper.

Tools: Cutting instruments such as a straight edged razor blade, a mat knife, or scissors.

Procedure: First build a pointed arch. It should be about six or eight inches high and eight or ten inches wide. Construct it as you did in the previous projects. Then you will need two halves of a semicircular arch. These should be made from a circle about ten inches in diameter. Glue the cubes together as you did before.

When you have constructed the pointed arch and the two half arches, build a high column two cubes square and rest each end of the pointed arch on top of them. Then build two more columns to support the half arches. They should be placed close enough to the columns supporting the pointed arch so that the half arches can reach from their supporting columns to the spring of the pointed arch as shown in the drawing.

You have now constructed a pointed arch and a flying buttress. The two should balance each other. If they do not, you must rearrange the construction of the various elements so that they do. For example, if the arch thrust of the pointed arch is stronger than the push of the flying buttress you may have to build the columns supporting the buttresses stronger and build them higher than the spring of the buttress. This is called a pinnacle. Its downward push helps to work against the side push of the buttress.

If the buttress is too strong, that is if it pushes in too hard against the pointed arch you might have to either add weight to the top of the pointed arch or make it wider so that it will push harder against the flying buttress.

This is exactly the means employed by the builders of Gothic cathedrals. They learned by experience the amount of thrust of the arch and then experimented to find means of counteracting it. The form of their arches, buttresses and pinnacles are the result of trial and error methods, like yours.

The foregoing project was a simplification of the solution of the Gothic arch. Pointed arches not only spanned straight across from column to column but also diagonally to the four columns forming a framework of pointed arch ribs. This arch framework was filled over with carefully fitted stones to complete the vaulting.

The next four drawings show how the semicircular and the Gothic arch compare with each other as they span directly across and diagonally from column to column.

The first drawing shows a semicircular arch as it would appear if we were facing it directly. The second drawing shows a semicircular arch viewed as it spans these same columns diagonally. The dotted lines are the first arch. You can see how much higher the second arch is than the first.

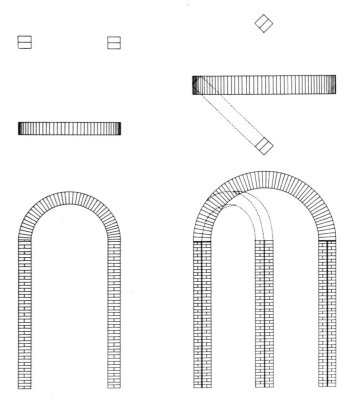

The third drawing shows a pointed arch spanning directly across from column to column and the fourth, the pointed arch, in diagonal span. The dotted lines show the first arch in comparison to the second. Both are the same height. This shows how the height of the pointed arch should be adjusted to suit the builder so that all of the arch ribs would meet in the center.

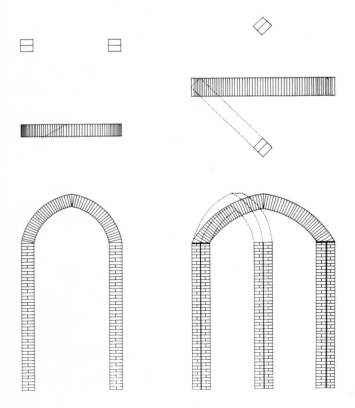

THE DOME

The dome is one of the most beautiful of masonry forms and one of the most difficult to construct. There are a number of methods used in building domes. No matter how the dome is finally constructed the difficulty begins with the fact that domes are usually placed over square rooms therefore the square must be converted to a circle.

There are two well known methods of doing this. The first is to build the circle within the square by bridging over the corners of the square with arches and then begin to gradually build a circular dome over the octagon. This creates a dome smaller than the square as can be seen in the drawings.

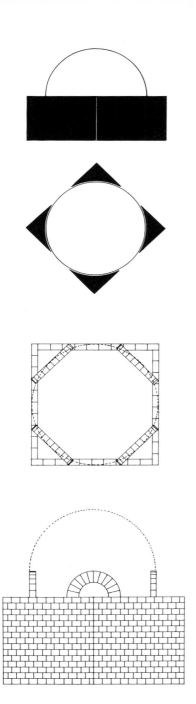

31

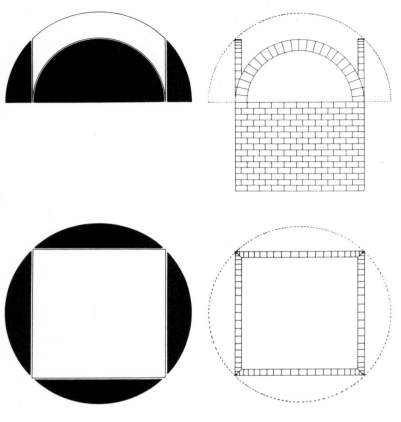

The other method is to set the square within the circle. This method can be visualized if we think of laying half of a rubber ball over a square so that its diameter touches the four corners of the square, then cutting off the sides of the rubber ball. What we have then is a dome that resembles a saucer supported on four concave triangles.

The saucer was sometimes left off and a cylinder called a drum inserted and a dome built on top of that.

However the dome was constructed the important thing for us to understand is how the dome itself is built.

Once a circle has been created the dome can be built by gradually making a smaller circle with each successive course (layer) of brick or stone to form a dome the way an igloo is built. As the bricks lean forward they brace themselves horizontally against each other much the same way that arch stones push together.

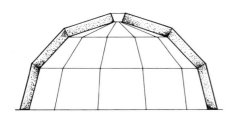

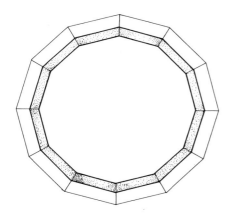

The drawing shows a small dome of sugar cubes so that you can see how the blocks work in forming the dome. This is the way the dome would look if it were cut in two vertically and horizontally. The blocks are beveled on all of their edges to work as an arch horizontally and vertically. The very top where the center stone (or keystone) of the arch would go has been left open. This would be impossible in an ordinary arch but it can be done because the dome also braces itself horizontally.

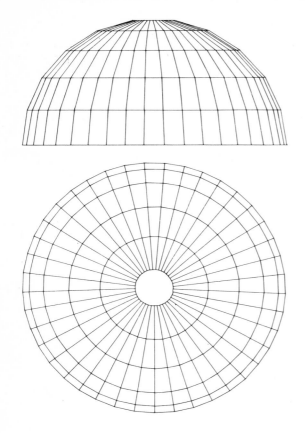

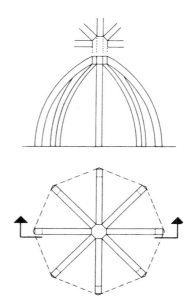

PROJECT 10 — Build a ribbed dome.

Materials: Two or three boxes of sugar cubes, white glue, cheap thin cardboard, waxed paper, sandpaper, two sheets of drawing paper.

Tools: Straight edged razor blade, mat knife or scissors.

Procedure: Draw an octagon on a piece of drawing paper or newspaper. (See drawing for method of constructing octagon.) Cover over the drawing with waxed paper. Make the octagon ten inches across.

The other drawings are of a side view and looking down on a much larger dome. Here you can see that the cubes begin to form a much more rounded circle. The smaller the stone, bricks or sugar cubes are in a dome in relation to its diameter the more round the dome appears. On very large domes they seem to be rounded themselves.

An exciting way to build a dome was that used by Brunelleschi when he built the dome of the Florence Cathedral. This is a dome built with ribs over an octagon almost like the pointed arches you saw before. It combines the arch and the dome together.

Let us see how hard it is to build.

Draw a section of the dome you wish to construct. A section is what the dome would look like if you cut through its center with a saw and were looking at one of the cut pieces. From this section construct an arch rib out of cardboard and build sugar cube ribs on top of it, the same way that you built arches. Sandpaper the cubes and glue them together.

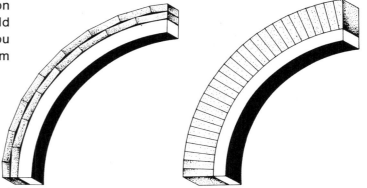

When you have built eight ribs put one at each corner of the octagon so that they will span from this corner up to the center of the octagon. Fill in between these ribs with sugar cubes sanding them to fit tightly against each other.

When you have done this you have constructed a dome of sugar cubes using the same method that was employed to build the great dome of Florence.

SCALE — PLAN — SECTION

Architects draw buildings to scale. This means drawing in one size to represent another. It is impossible to make a drawing the same size as the entire building, so one-quarter of an inch, one-eighth of an inch or one-half of an inch may be used to represent one foot. The building can then be drawn in its entirety in miniature. This is called drawing to scale. The scale of the drawing is the unit of measure that has been selected to represent one foot.

Plans and sections are also made of the building. These are drawings of the building, drawn to scale, that represent what the building would look like if it were cut in half. The plan is a cut horizontally and the section is a cut vertically.

It is often very important to show exactly where the drawing of the building has been cut for the plan or section. When we wish to show this we use a heavy line with arrows attached. In this instance the arrow is not the direction of a force but the direction we are looking after we have theoretically cut the building at this place. If you think of the arrows as two eyes looking in the direction they are pointing you will remember what these marks mean.

HARMONY

There are other systems of balance in architecture besides the physical balances we have been working with. The visual relationships between the parts of the building also form a system of balance. The architects of the buildings before modern times were very interested in this balance. They considered it of greater importance than structure.

These architects thought that harmony, or symmetry, as they termed this balance could be as logically determined as structure. They analyzed and defined the laws of beauty geometrically. They based their calculations on the geometry and proportions of a well formed man.

Whether beautiful architecture can be arrived at by logical calculation or whether it can only result from undefinable intuition is a question as old as art itself. However it cannot be denied that some very beautiful buildings were designed logically employing the principles of symmetry and harmony. These concepts are therefore an integral element in the joy of building.

MEASUREMENT

When we use a ruler to measure an object, we are determining its size in relation to a given, commonly accepted set of measurements. The two commonly used of these measuring systems are the metric, which is based on a set infinitesimal dimension of the earth's meridian, and the foot and inch system, which is based upon the foot and a portion of the human thumb. Both systems are simple devices for standardizing measurement by relating size to a universally accepted scale.

The ancients sought to use measurements not only to establish size but also to create harmony. By this they meant a relationship between the sizes of the measuring units themselves. As Vitruvius, a Roman architect living in the second century A.D. said, "Proportion is a correspondence among the measures of the members of an entire work, and the whole to a certain part selected as standard".

The method used by the builders before modern architecture was to select a dimension and measure the entire building in terms of this dimension, thereby establishing a "correspondence among its members". For example the diameter of a column was used as a basic unit. Instead of thinking of the column diameter as two feet wide and its height as sixteen feet high, its dimension was considered to be one diameter to eight diameters. The entire temple then was designed using the column diameter as a measuring stick.

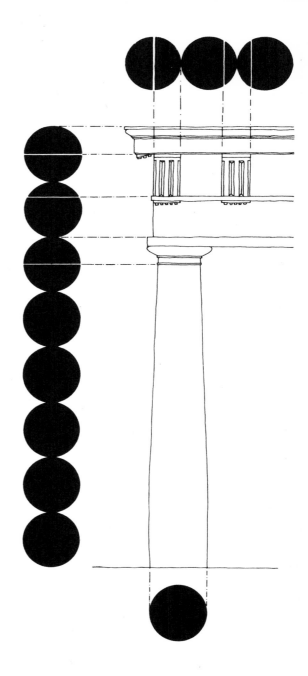

Practically, the system had the advantage of containing a measuring system within itself. No standardized ruler in feet or meters was needed. Any size column diameter selected could be used to dimension the building. On the other hand there was no way of telling someone just exactly how big anything was without showing them the exact column diameter. A column diameter in Athens was not necessarily the same as a column diameter in Delphi, but this was unimportant to the Greeks as long as both temples were harmoniously proportioned.

Among the oldest and best known harmonic systems is that of the Golden Section. Here a simple idea establishes harmony between two dimensions. The theory is to divide a given line so that the smaller part will be to the larger as the larger is to the whole. The relationship can be approximated by the series 3:5:8:13:21:34:55 . . . in which any number is the sum of the two preceding (3 + 5 = 8, 5 + 8 = 13, 8 + 13 = 21, etc.). The geometric device which will produce this system is constructed by dividing a square in half vertically, using the diagonal of the half as the radius of an arc to the base of the square. This dimension is then used to construct another square. This series of dimensions will be exact measurements of the Golden Section instead of approximations as the 3:5:8 . . . series are. You can verify that each segment of the line constructed with the Golden Section squares is the sum of the two sections preceding it by measurement.

The Golden Section is only one system of proportions. Systems can be devised upon the squaring of a number, counting by two's, etc. Such systems have been used throughout the ages.

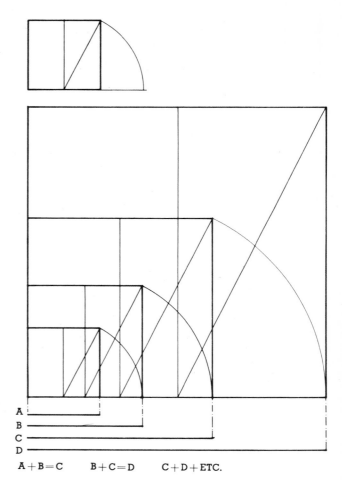

A + B = C   B + C = D   C + D + ETC.

In the two opposite drawings one of the squares has its sides divided by the square of 2, the other has been divided into approximate golden section dimensions with the 3:5:8:13, etc. series of numbers. Note that in both instances all of the squares and rectangles within the large squares are visually related to each other.

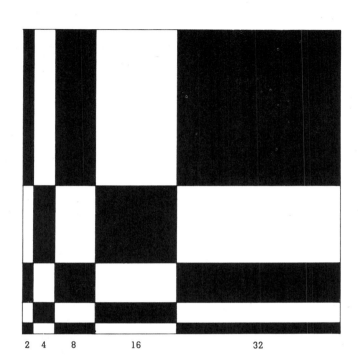

2 4 8 16 32

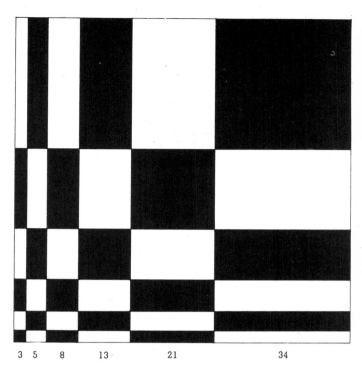

3 5 8 13 21 34

PROJECT 11 — Make a modular game.

Materials: Cutting tool, scissors or mat knife, ruler, and straight edge, paper (2 colors).

Procedure: Mark the two adjacent edges of both sheets of paper in the progression, 3:5:8:13:... etc. until you come to the edge or near the edge of the paper. The number of marks you make will depend on the basic unit of measure you select, sixteenths of an inch, eighths, quarters, etc. When you have marked the edge of the paper draw straight lines parallel to the edge at these points as shown. You will have a series of squares and rectangles. Cut the papers on these lines.

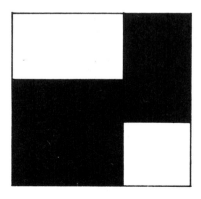

3 — 5 — 8 — 13 — 21 — 34

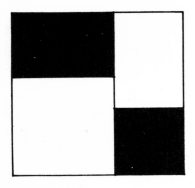

2 — 4 — 8 — 16 — 32

If we arrange the various squares and rectangles into smaller squares and rectangles using the two different colored papers we will find that their various elements form harmonious relationships.

This simple geometric device is not the answer to the problem of design. Even Le Corbusier, who invented the game did not claim that the modular would automatically create good design. He stated that it would make bad design more difficult.

MAN THE MEASURE OF ALL THINGS

Now that we have devised a method of creating symmetrical and harmonious systems of measurement we can take another step. We can relate these measurements to man. There are a number

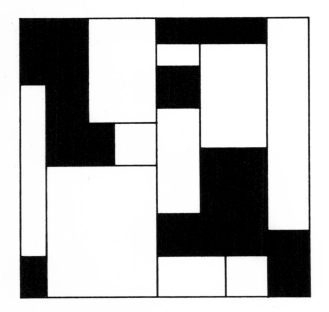

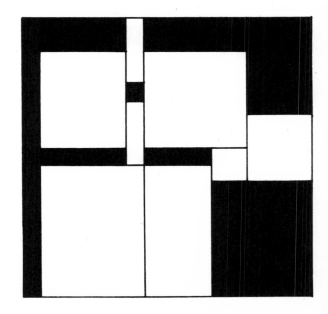

of good reasons for doing this. Primary among them is that if we assume that buildings are built for people, it makes good sense to have a system of measurement that relates to the people who will be using the buildings. Sizes of doors, windows, rooms, hallways, in short, all of the parts would be related to man's proportions both physically and visually.

In past ages man was conceived of as the measure of all things. In medieval times Villard de Honnecourt transferred the geometry of the human face to a building's facade. During the Renaissance, man's proportions were used to determine the dimensions of cathedrals. Let us see just how big man, the measure of all things, really is.

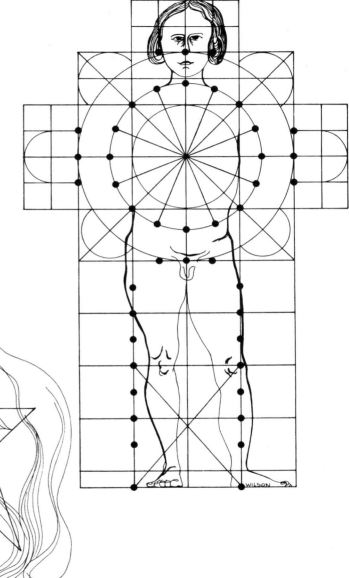

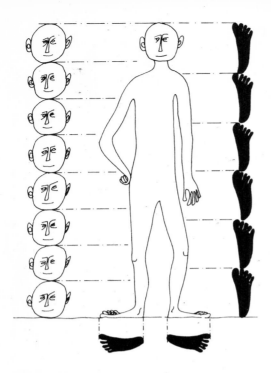

late to the rest of his body? For example, how many of his foot sizes is he high, how many of his own hand sizes is he high?

Do not use rulers to make these measurements. Mark off the size of the person's body you are measuring on a piece of cardboard, string, or paper and compare with other parts of their body, measure in terms of hands, foreheads, forearms, etc., not in the inches of a ruler.

Once you have worked out a scale of human dimensions you are ready to decide how high a table should be in open hands, heads, forearms,

PROJECT 12 — Measuring man.

Materials: A strip of paper about six feet long which you can use as a measuring tape. Several friends (as many as will stand still while you conduct this research).

Procedure: Measure them to find the proportion of their parts in relation to each other. Use the paper strip to mark the dimensions.

1 — Is the open hand, from the wrist to the tip of the middle finger, the same as the distance from the chin to the root of the hair?

2 — What is the relation to the other parts of the body of the dimension of the head from the chin to the tip of the crown?

3 — What is the relation of the length of the forearm to other parts of the body?

4 — How does the length of a person's foot re-

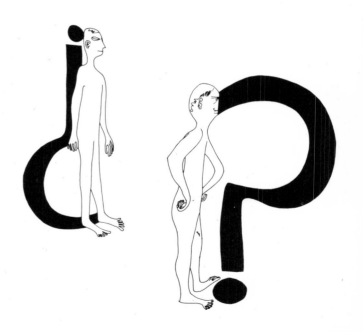

etc. Determine how high chairs and other articles of furniture should be to accommodate the human body. For example, how high should a door be, how high up a wall should a window be located and how high should it extend over a person's head. We can now design all of the room dimensions that would be the most comfortable for human occupancy in terms of human scale. You might compare the dimensions you decide are the best against those of the room you are in. Do you think that they are the best proportion for a human being?

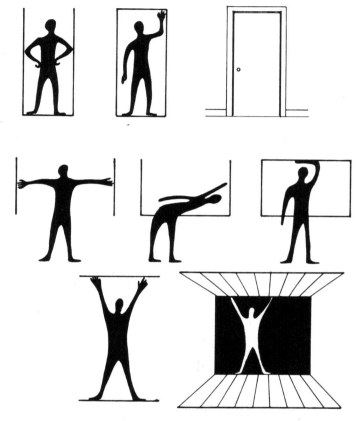

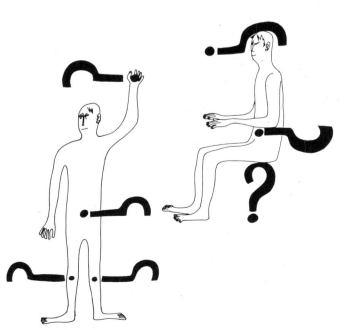

HARMONIOUS PROPORTION IN RELATION TO HUMAN SCALE

We have now found two measuring systems. The first is based upon dimensions related to each other which create harmony of proportion. The second is based upon the proportions of the human body. Combining these two systems is a very old architectural problem.

Le Corbusier solved this problem with two systems of measurement. One series (. . . 27, 43, 70, 113, 183, etc.) and the other the series of (. . . 86, 140, 226, etc.). The first series gives the position of the man's hand at his side when standing (86), the position of his fingertips with arm upraised (226) etc. the second series positions the man's navel at (113) and the top of his head at (183). Note that these figures are in centimeters and will not translate evenly into inches.

Combining these two series of related dimensions Le Corbusier found it possible to use them to measure the human body in various positions. He then used these figures to dimension the height of chair seats, position arm rests, tell how high a doorway should be and how wide. In short he could dimension his building to human scale with harmonious dimensions.

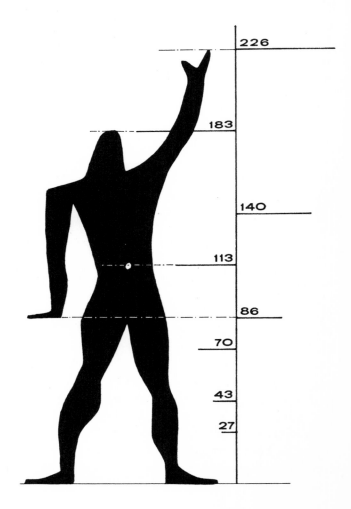

PROJECT 13 — Build a small, harmoniously proportioned building.

Materials: Several boxes of sugar cubes, cheap light cardboard, white glue, waxed paper, sketch pad, pencil, the scale you have made from the human figure and the small scale figure to measure with (described below).

Tools: Straight edged razor blade, mat knife or scissors.

Procedure: Build a small structure out of sugar cubes that will combine what you know about building with what you have learned about harmonious proportions and the human figure.

First you should select a unit in the same way the Greeks used their column dimension as the basic unit of measurement.

Before you begin, you should establish a scale to have an idea of the type of space you are creating in relation to the people who will be using it. You can use a sugar cube as the basis of this scale. Pretend that the height of the cube, which is about three-quarters of an inch represents one foot. Using this dimension, find a photograph in a magazine or a newspaper that is five and one-half or six sugar cubes high. Paste it on a piece of cardboard then cut out around its edges. Make the cardboard a little longer than the figure so that it can be bent at right angles as a stand. This will be your model to compare your building with human scale.

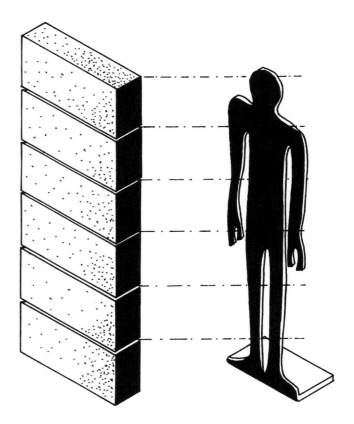

Next using the small cardboard figure make a scale in heads or hands or feet or elbows as you did with a life sized person in the last project. This will be your ruler. Try to relate all of the dimensions to each other. For example, if a wall is 34 heads long perhaps it should be 21 heads high and the doorway should be five heads wide. As you will recognize, these are figures taken from the 3:5:8:13:21:34: ... series of dimensions.

Make it complete with walls, columns and a roof that is arched, corbelled, or combination of the two. Since this is a very complicated idea, it is best to build a very simple structure like a one room studio instead of trying to design an entire house.

PART 2
MODERN ARCHITECTURE

Up until now you have experimented with structural problems which were characteristic of old architecture. These involved structural problems of buildings with strong enough materials, but with weak joints. They used the pull of gravity to balance their masses against each other to create stable structures.

The beginning of what we now call modern architecture occurred a little over a hundred years ago. Yet, during this comparatively short span of architectural history there have been more changes in the appearance of buildings, due to structural innovation, than during the millenniums following the erection of Stonehenge.

Modern architecture came about with the invention of strong materials and strong joints. Building with strong materials can reverse the appearance of gravity bound structures. Many of the ideas that modern architecture uses today have been known for centuries and were used sparingly in old architecture. For example the Romans and the Renaissance builders used trusses. Suspension structures have been used by primitive cultures of Africa and South America long before the Europeans came to these places. The Romans used concrete and, of course, the beam and tie rods were used for centuries. However, with the manufacture of steel and concrete these structural forms became commonplace and began to change the appearance of buildings.

In modern architecture the art of design and the science of construction meet in the working of materials. An improvement in a material or its method of manufacture provides new design dimensions. Instead of building by experiment we now have a building science that will predict what will happen before we build the building.

Some of the things that make modern architecture look the way it does is our ability to construct a continuous structure of one material, or to join

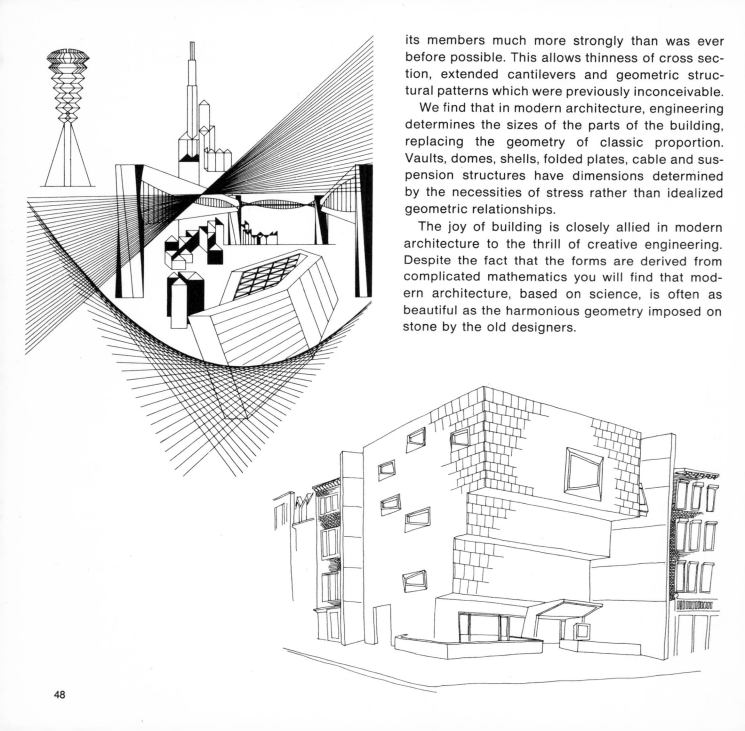

its members much more strongly than was ever before possible. This allows thinness of cross section, extended cantilevers and geometric structural patterns which were previously inconceivable.

We find that in modern architecture, engineering determines the sizes of the parts of the building, replacing the geometry of classic proportion. Vaults, domes, shells, folded plates, cable and suspension structures have dimensions determined by the necessities of stress rather than idealized geometric relationships.

The joy of building is closely allied in modern architecture to the thrill of creative engineering. Despite the fact that the forms are derived from complicated mathematics you will find that modern architecture, based on science, is often as beautiful as the harmonious geometry imposed on stone by the old designers.

THE BEAM

The simple beam has been used since the beginning of time. It was employed extensively in timber and stone construction by the old builders. However, how the beam actually works was never understood until comparatively recently. That is why we are discussing it in this section.

The function of the masonry column, the wall, and the arch which we previously studied with our sugar cubes, was to balance compressive loads and channel them to their supports.

A beam does something altogether different. Beams can be simply defined as devices that transfer vertical loads horizontally along their length to the beam supports. It does this by withstanding bending stresses which are a combination of both tensile and compressive forces.

The following project will demonstrate this principle.

PROJECT 14 — Build a simple device to find compression and tension in a beam.

Materials: A thin rectangular piece of soft wood like pine. It should be about eighteen inches long, one-quarter of an inch thick and three-quarters of an inch wide.

Procedure: Put the piece of wood between two books with the one-quarter edge up. Pile books upon it until it bends about one inch out of line. Remove the books. Cut a thin notch three-eighths of an inch deep (half way through) in the three-quarter inch width. Cut the notch at the center of the beam. Put this cut edge up and load the wood with books as you did before. You will notice that the wood bends but does not break. The cut notch closes up as its sides push against each other.

Remove the books and turn the wood over with the notch at the bottom. You will observe when you begin replacing the books on the beam that the notch opens up. The beam is only half as effective as it was before. You can see that the top of the beam withstands compressive or pushing forces (the notch closes) and the bottom withstands tensile or pulling forces (the notch opens).

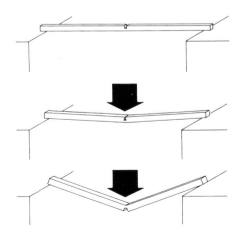

Another very important property of the beam is that its shape contributes to its strength. A flat piece of cardboard (which we will pretend is a beam) one-sixteenth of an inch thick and one inch wide and twelve inches long will not support its own weight lying flat between two books. However if this cardboard is turned on edge it will hold a considerable amount of weight, if we can prevent it from moving sideways. This proves that the beam is stronger or weaker depending on how it is placed in the building.

It can also be shown that the most stress in a beam is at its top and bottom edges. Almost everyone is familiar with the I beam used in construction. This shape concentrates most of the beam's material (usually steel) at the very top and the very bottom of the beam where the stresses are the greatest.

To illustrate how the distribution of the beam's material affects the beam's strength, let us work out the following project.

PROJECT 15 — Build models to compare beam shapes.

Materials: Light cheap cardboard, white glue, waxed paper.
Tools: Straight edged razor blade, mat knife or scissors.
Procedure: This will be a project in two parts. You will make two beams with the same amount of material and see which will hold the most.

First you should make a simple I beam. It should be about eighteen inches long and two inches deep with flanges (top and bottom pieces of the I) three-quarters of an inch wide. Cut out the three strips of cardboard. One of these should be eighteen inches long and two inches wide, the other two should be eighteen inches long and three-

quarters of an inch wide. Glue the three-quarter-inch pieces to the two inch piece to form an I and allow to dry. Don't forget the waxed paper to protect your working surface.

Now you will make a more complicated beam. Cut out a piece of cardboard about twenty-two inches long and two inches wide. Then cut it as shown in the drawing. Move the two parts apart

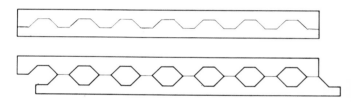

and glue them so the center is a series of openings. When this has dried cut it down to eighteen inches. Then glue two three-quarter inch strips to either edge as you did with the simple I beam.

When the second beam has dried out you can put the two beams between two tables and load them with an identical amount of weight to see which will hold the most.

Obviously both beams are identical except for the distribution of their material. The second beam is much deeper than the first. From this you can learn that the deeper the beam the more it will support.

If the flanges buckle when the beams are loaded you can place small triangular pieces of cardboard against the flange and the web (the upright leg of the I) to hold them in place as shown in the drawing.

Do you think that you can invent a better shape for a beam now that you have an idea of how a beam works? The object of the next project is to design a beam shape using the least amount of material that will support the most weight.

Do not forget that the maximum stresses are at the top and the bottom of the beam and that the beam must be restrained from moving laterally.

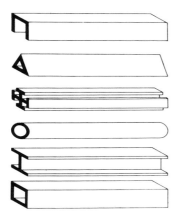

PROJECT 16 — Can you invent a beam?

Materials: Cheap thin cardboard or heavy paper, waxed paper and white glue.

Tools: Straight edged razor blade, mat knife or scissors.

Testing Equipment: Postal scale or other sensitive weighing device, scissors, and a weight that can be used for testing the beam. Lead fish sinkers are excellent for this. They should be tied to a loop of cord passed over the beam. The weight can then be moved from one end of the beam to its center and you can observe the difference in deflection (bending) as the weights move along the beam. As you will remember the force increases with distance. At what point on the beam will there be the most force acting upon it?

If you are going to compare beam shapes then both beams should be made out of the same cardboard or paper. The number of fish weights and how heavy they are will depend upon the material you use.

If you are using heavy paper which is thinner than light cardboard, you need not make your beam as long, about twelve or fourteen inches should be long enough. If you make it out of light cardboard make it about eighteen to twenty inches and if you should happen to use heavy cardboard make it twenty-four to thirty inches long.

Procedure: After you have designed and constructed your beam shape, place it between two supports for testing and move the fish weights along its length to see how strong it is. If the beam holds then take off the fish weights and weigh the beam on the scale.

If you feel that you have too much material in the beam you can cut out parts of it with scissors or the razor blade, test it with weights again and then see how much it weighs.

If the beam fails, note carefully how it does so. If it wrinkles it is failing from compression, if it tears it is failing from tension. You might redesign it strengthening the areas for either of these stresses and test again.

THE COLUMN REVISITED

You found earlier with sugar cubes that the short column has comparatively few problems, but that as the column becomes longer its structural problems multiply. The column must be kept from bending sideways and, as with the beam, certain proportions are better than others to prevent this. A flat piece of paper stood vertically will not support its own weight, yet the same piece of paper can be creased to hold objects many times heavier than itself.

You will now experiment with paper columns to find what happens to them when they are supporting weight.

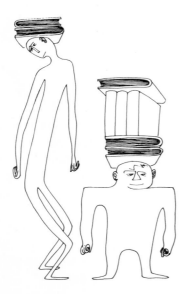

PROJECT 17 — Making paper columns.

Materials: Brown wrapping paper such as that used in stores to wrap packages, waxed paper, broom handle, white glue.

Procedure: Wrap pieces of waxed paper around the broom handle to prevent glue from sticking to it. Cut out pieces of brown paper six, eight, ten, twelve and sixteen inches long and wide enough to go around the broom handle. Wrap the pieces of paper around the handle over the waxed paper and glue their edges together to make paper cylinders of different lengths.

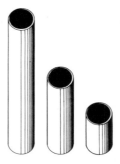

These paper cylinders represent small columns. It will be found if you place books on top of these cylinders that the shorter ones will support more than the longer.

As the longest cylinder collapses it will probably crease on one side and fall over. This shows that it is failing by bending in the same fashion as a beam. If the very short columns are overloaded, they will be crushed.

Can you devise methods of strengthening these columns against these two forms of stress by gluing additional pieces of wrapping paper to them?

This brings us to our next project.

PROJECT 18 — Invent a column shape.

Materials: Cheap thin cardboard or heavy paper, waxed paper and white glue.

Tools: Razor blade, mat knife or scissors.

Procedure: Invent a column shape as you invented a shape for the beam. Use the knowledge you have gained in the previous project.

Determine the column height in relation to the kind of material you are using. If you are using paper, the column should be shorter; if heavy cardboard, make it longer.

Glue square pieces of paper or cardboard to the top and the bottom of the column so that it will stand flat on your working surface and so that it can hold the weights you put on it more easily.

You may try the same thing with the column that you did with the beam. It can be weighed and parts can be cut away to see if they are adding to its strength.

Contrast the beam shape with the shape of the column and see how they differ. Why do you think this is?

COLUMN AND BEAM CONNECTIONS

The ability of both the column and the beam to support loads depends upon their connection to the structure. They may be fastened to the building with either a hinged or a fixed connection. A hinge, as its name implies, allows for movement. The solid, or rigid connection, holds the members rigidly so they do not move.

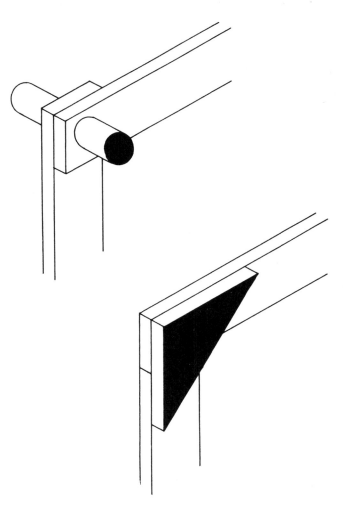

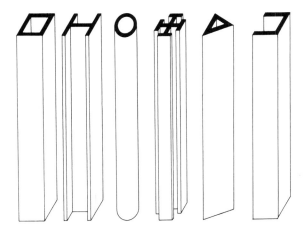

PROJECT 19 — Testing the difference between a pin and a rigid connection.

Materials: A thirty-six inch piece of wood about three-eighths of an inch square, two clamps, a ruler and a yardstick.

Procedure: Place the wood between two desks or tables with a two inch overlap onto the table at either end. Lay the yardstick next to the wood then place a weight at the center of the wood. Take a ruler and measure the difference between the bent surface of the wood and the yardstick. This bending is called deflection when it occurs in a beam.

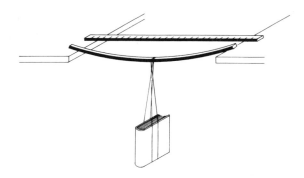

Take the weight off the wood and clamp the two overlapping ends securely to the table. Put the same weight back on the wood and measure the amount of deflection as you did before.

It will be found that the wood deflected less when its ends were restrained (held by the clamps) than it did when the ends were left free to move on the table.

Take a flexible strip of plastic, such as a plastic ruler, place it between your fingers and push. The harder you push the more it will curve. Both ends of the ruler are free to move. This approximates a hinged joint. Now if you take the same ruler, grasp the ends and twist, it will bend but not as much. This is the solid or rigid connection. It transfers some of the bending stresses to the supporting structure as you could feel in your fingers. The kind of curves the ruler made under these conditions are also very different. With a hinged connection the curve was a simple either upward or downward arc, but with the rigid connection the curves are both upward and downward.

Let us measure the effects of the two kinds of connections.

The same experiment could be made with the wood upright to simulate a column. This requires a more complicated arrangement to hold it in place. However, the results would be the same. The restrained wood column would deflect less than the column whose ends were free to move.

LOOKING AT COLUMN SIZES

You have seen how important the shape and the connection of a column is in the preceding projects. The factors that will cause a column to fail are the relationship between its shape, its height, its fastening and the loads imposed upon it.

If we assume that we are within the safe ratio of column height to shape and connection to load then all we must consider is the size of the column in relation to the load it is supporting. In comparing two columns, the column with double the cross-sectional area will carry double the load.

If we look at the drawing, which is a plan of a series of columns, it can be seen that the cross-

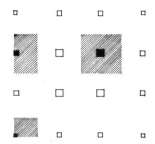

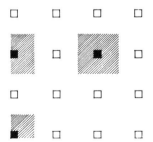

hatched area indicates the amount of floor load each column is supporting. Note that the corner columns carry a load which is only half that carried by the perimeter columns and that the perimeter columns carry only half the load of the in-

terior columns. In the second drawings the columns are roughly the size they would be if they were sized in relation to the loads they are supporting.

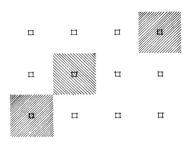

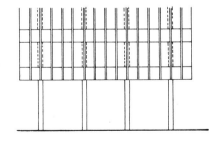

In the third drawing you see two cantilevers. Here it can be observed that by projecting the building out over the columns the same load is carried by the corner columns as those in the interior of the building.

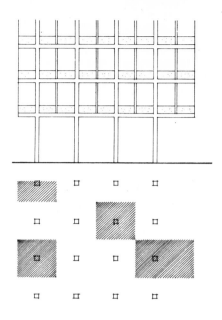

PROPORTION IN RELATION TO LOADS

Look at the adjacent elevation and plan drawing. Does one of the cantilevers look wrong? If so, which and why? Now look at the plan and find the answer.

From these observations we may determine that the size of a column should be proportionate to the loads it supports. This is the way we expect columns to look in buildings. If they do not, we experience a sense of uneasiness. Or we find the building dull and uninteresting.

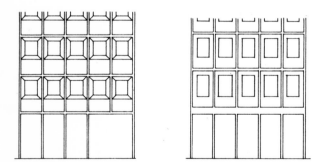

For example look at this drawing. Here we have two different building elevations and both of them have something wrong with them. What is it?

It is easy to see that the loss of the column without increasing the dimension of the beam (its depth) to carry the extra load is illogical. In the other drawing we ask ourselves why it was necessary for the first beam to be so heavy when all of the above columns are supporting thin beams?

When we see incongruities like these we become distrustful of the entire structural logic of the building. The discovery of the structural system of a modern building from the information given to you on its facade can be a fascinating game. Careful examination reveals the building's secrets to you.

THE MODERN MODULE

Modern buildings are the work of machines. The high-rise steel building uses the structural principle of the beam and the column but endlessly multiplied.

Machine manufacture of parts of buildings makes it necessary for the parts to be of standard sizes or modular. As a consequence, modern architects use the machine module just as the old architects used the diameter of a column as the basic unit of measurement. However they are forced to be more practical than aesthetic.

If a building's module is four feet and four inches, the window mullions (members between the windows) would be spaced at this distance. Two

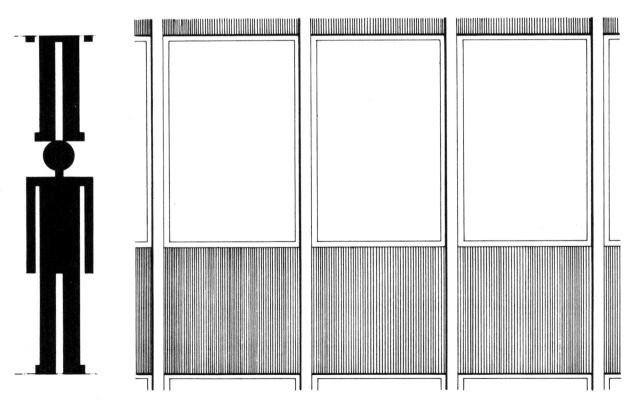

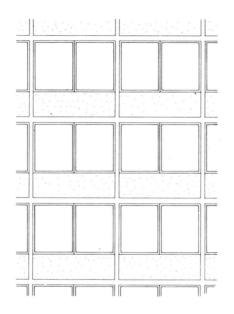

of these modules would be enough for a small office, three for an important executive and four for the office of the company president. Column spacing would follow this modular measurement with column centers at twenty-one feet and eight inches or five window mullion spaces apart.

This measuring system dictates the building's interior planning. Mechanical equipment such as air-conditioning, ceiling lighting and electrical outlets are all designed to these basic dimensions.

The modern building has become a standardized combination of components which are assembled like one huge erector set. This is the reason that modern buildings look the way they do. They are saying in their repetitive geometric facades that they house a module, and that people will be fitted into this interior system.

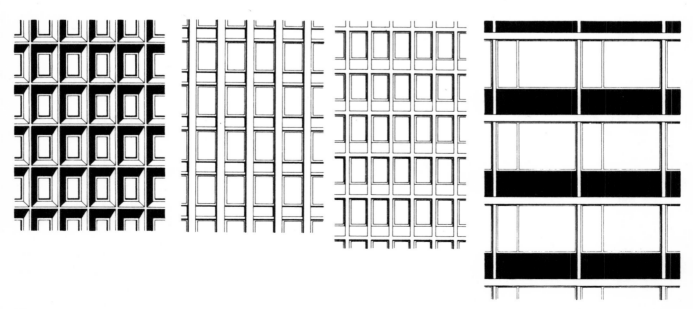

STRUCTURE FOLLOWING THE GEOMETRY OF STRESS

In modern architecture, machine made parts and engineered geometry replace the classic harmonies. To understand the forms of modern architecture we must understand engineering principles.

To illustrate stress and geometry we might examine the following forms of simple bending trans-

lated into structure. The drawing shows a man pushing against another whose feet are held to the ground by weights. The second drawing shows a man extending himself perpendicular to a wall. In both instances the form of bending stress, if it were drawn, would be in the shape of a triangle, beginning at nothing at its apex and ending with a stress of maximum magnitude at the base.

It would be logical to design a structural member in the form of a triangle to withstand these types of stress. This is, of course, a simplification. There are other stresses to consider besides the bending stresses described here. Where bending

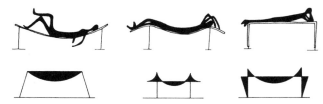

is the most important consideration, this would be a logical way of designing these structural members.

Let us look at a few other examples of the same idea. A man lying on a board between two unconnected supports, a man lying on a board that overhangs its supports, and a man lying on a table whose legs are rigidly connected to its top. In each instance the bending stress diagram would be as shown below the drawing.

It can be seen that these different forms of stress produce entirely different bending conditions. In each instance structures have been designed that reflect these principles and in many of them their forms are remarkably like the diagrams shown. This is what is meant when we say a building is following the lines of stress in its design. Here the engineering principles are responsible for the form of the building.

We might observe that these forms of stress might produce buildings with profiles almost opposite in appearance to those we have experimented with in old architecture. Modern materials with their ability to make strong joints transfer stresses entirely differently than the old masonry buildings which depended upon gravity alone for their stability.

Instead of the pyramidal piling of masonry the base of a modern building may do just the opposite by coming to a hinged point.

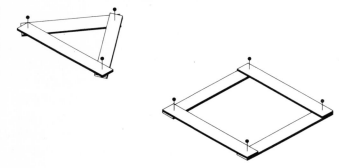

Let us experiment with some of these principles to see how they work. We will begin with the triangle. You have seen that beams which span long distances must be very deep. The arch, although materially economic, is difficult to hold in place high in the air and masonry is very heavy. The truss, which is an ingenious arrangement wherein the members are arranged so that they function in either tension or compression without bending stresses, is a better answer as you will see in the next project.

The triangle is the only geometric figure that cannot change shape without altering its sides by either shortening or lengthening.

The triangle is a geometric figure that will hold its shape even though its three joints are hinged. To test this, take three pieces and four pieces of cardboard of equal length and pin them together as shown in the drawing. You will find that the triangle will hold its shape when pushed but that the square will become a parallelogram. Therefore, if we build a structure composed entirely of triangles it will be very rigid.

If you are going to use triangles in a truss you should find which members are in compression and which in tension. This is important since a tension member could be much lighter. You will find in the following experiments that a thin thread or string can be used instead of a much heavier piece of wood.

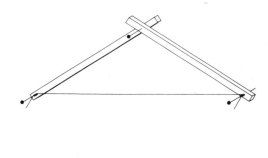

PROJECT 20 — Build a truss.

Materials: Four pieces of balsa wood (buy these in a model-making shop), soft pine could be used as an alternative. The wood should be one-quarter of an inch square and about twenty inches long. If you use heavier pieces of wood it will not be as much of a challenge, nor as much fun to solve. #50 sewing thread and white glue.

Tools: Small toothed saw, mat knife, or razor blade.

Procedure: Place two desks eighteen inches apart. Place the four pieces of wood between the desks and find a book that is heavy enough to make them bend but not break. Take the book off the wood and invent a truss using as little wood and thread

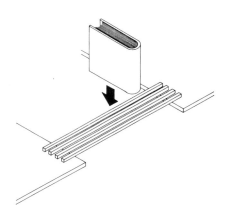

as you can to support the same book. You might make several of these to find which one works the best with the least material.

After you have invented a truss you should be ready to build a space frame. This is a marvelous invention which is like a truss in all directions, or a number of trusses connected.

This is one of the most economical structures, in terms of material, known to modern architecture. You will see why after you have built one.

PROJECT 21 — Build a space frame.

Materials: Two boxes of round toothpicks, white glue, waxed paper.

Tools: Knife or cutting instrument.

Before we proceed: A WORD ABOUT GLUING TOOTHPICKS

This will take time and is delicate work. White glue is the best to use, but it takes time to set. An excellent way to begin is to lay the toothpicks on the waxed paper and glue them into triangles or whatever form you wish to make. When the glue has set, then prop other toothpicks into the position that you want and glue these to the original triangles.

When the white glue dries it will shrink. Where you have used too much, and it is very difficult to use just the right amount, you will find that the excess forms a rubbery mass which can be easily cut away.

Sometimes you can make the glue stick better if you pour it out on the waxed paper and let it set a little before using. Use it as it begins to congeal.

The toothpicks will not meet perfectly since their points are sharp and they are not all exactly the same length. This does not matter. They can be slightly trimmed when the glue has set.

It is best to wait until the next day to test your structure when you are sure that the glue is thoroughly dry. You will find that toothpicks are extremely strong when used carefully. You could if you were very careful build a structure that you could stand on.

Procedure: Your aim is to make a construction of toothpicks that will span two feet between supports and hold up ten pounds of books. The toothpicks are to be glued together using as few toothpicks as possible. Do not cut the toothpicks; use them as they come out of the box.

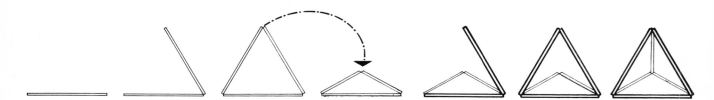

The best method to build a space frame, you will find, is to construct triangles as shown in the drawing. The drawing shows the construction of a tetrahedron (a polyhedron with four sides). First construct a triangle by gluing three toothpicks together, then lay the triangle flat and build a pyramid of toothpicks from each of its corners. You will find that this is a very rigid and very strong structure. If you continue to use this principle you will be obtaining the maximum strength from the toothpicks. However, you will find this is almost impossible to do if you wish to construct certain shapes. When you depart from triangulation to construct a square, it will not be as stable as the triangle. When this happens, you can glue tooth-picks across the corner of the square to strengthen it, as shown in the drawing.

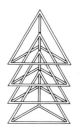

When you have made the structure, hold it in your hand and gently squeeze. If it does not feel rigid but moves in your hand look for the configurations that move. You will find that these invariably are not triangulated. Glue toothpicks across their corners to make them rigid.

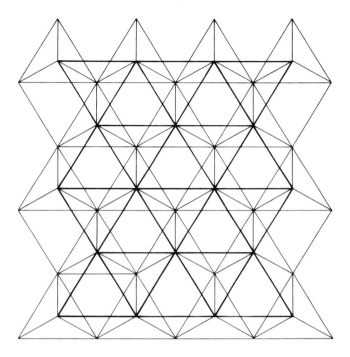

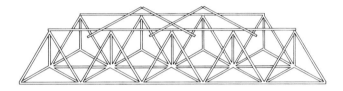

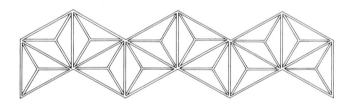

Now that we have found how well the triangles work let us compare them to a structure of rigid frames. This is a construction the joints of which are so strongly fastened that they transfer bending stresses to adjacent members. This is the opposite principle of the pin jointed triangle.

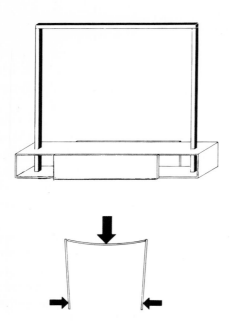 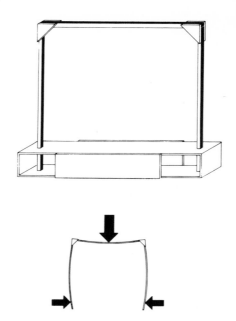

PROJECT 22 — Build a rigid frame.

Materials: Six pieces of balsa wood or soft pine, each twelve inches long and one-quarter of an inch square, cardboard, waxed paper and white glue.

Tools: Straight edged razor blade, mat knife or scissors.

Procedure: Build two frames as shown in the drawings to hold two pieces of wood upright. The cardboard frames are made to hold the bottom of the wooden uprights or columns so that they do not spread apart when a load is placed on the horizontal or beam member supported by the columns. It should be strong enough to hold the wood and also allow you to see how the columns move at the bottom. In one, lay a piece of balsa wood across the top and, in the other rigidly connect the top piece to the two legs by gluing a small triangular square of cardboard at the joint, as shown on the drawing. Now place weight upon both of these frames and see how they react. In the unconnected frame the legs will move out as the top piece bends in a downward arc. In the second instance the weight will force the top to bend but the legs will also bend showing that some of the bending stress have been transferred to them.

If we lift the braced structure out of its frame it will deflect entirely differently under loading. The legs will move out instead of bending.

Let us construct a truss of rigid frames.

PROJECT 23 — Build a truss of rigid frames.

Materials: Thin cheap cardboard, white glue, waxed paper.
Tools: Cutting instrument.
Procedure: Make a truss out of cardboard as shown in the drawing. It should be about twenty-

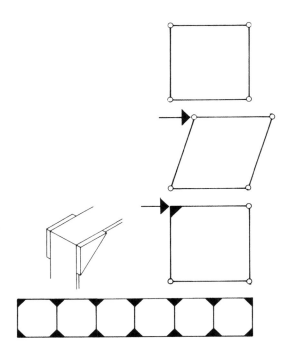

four inches long and about three inches high. Cut the strips three-quarters of an inch wide. Make rigid joints by gluing small triangles of cardboard where the upright truss members meet the top and bottom of the truss.

Test this truss by loading as you did the triangular truss. You will find that if you cut a member, the truss will probably fail. If it does not it will mean that it has been built stronger than it need be.

CONCRETE

Concrete is a hardened liquid stone. It has no more and sometimes less strength than many of the harder stones. However when concrete is liquid, steel can be placed in it to give the concrete strength in tension making it far superior in strength to any natural stone.

From our observation of the simple beam we will remember that the top is in compression and the bottom in tension. The steel in a concrete beam is placed low in the beam in the tensile stress area. As we know, stone acts well in compression without any help so the top of the concrete beam takes care of itself.

The same practice is followed in building columns. From our experience with columns, we know that they usually fail by bending or buckling which begins at their outside edges. Where would you place the steel in round concrete columns to withstand these tendencies?

PRESTRESSED CONCRETE

One of the most recent developments in construction is the introduction of systems of tensioning material during construction to counteract the loads that will be placed on the structure when it is completed. This is almost like having one person on the seesaw to begin with so that when the other takes his place they will be balanced.

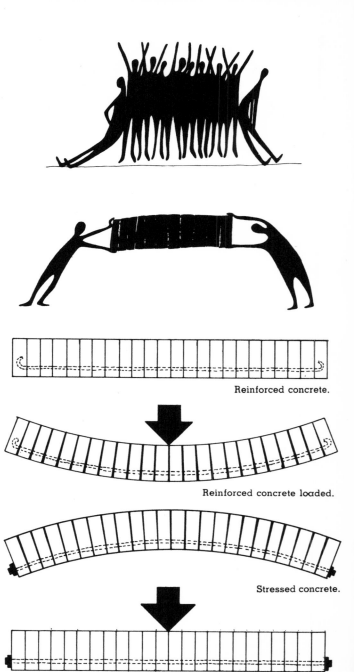

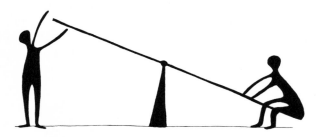

The idea is quite simple. We know that if we wish to lift a number of books stacked horizontally we must exert enough horizontal pressure against them to hold them together. This is part of the idea of how concrete is stressed. As we have seen in reinforced concrete, steel tenons have to be introduced to give the concrete strength in tension. In stressed concrete the steel is pulled tight to exert pressure as we do when lifting books. Since the steel is placed low in the beam as shown in the drawing, it reverses the tensions that are exerted in a normal beam. The steel places the bottom of the beam in compression and the top in tension. In reality the beam bends slightly upward instead of downwards. When loads are put on the beam it comes back to its normal straightness, taking the tension out of the top of the beam and placing the entire beam in compression which is the way the concrete works best.

This is a very easy theory to illustrate.

Reinforced concrete.

Reinforced concrete loaded.

Stressed concrete.

Stressed concrete loaded.

PROJECT 24 — Build a prestressed beam.

Materials: Set of small rectangular two inch blocks cut from a long piece of soft wood one-half inch square. Two rubber bands large enough to go around the blocks.

Procedure: Place the blocks in a row as shown in the drawing. Put a rubber band around them in their center. Using the blocks as a beam, supported by two books or between two desks, place loads upon it. Remove the weights and put a rubber band toward the bottom edge of the blocks so that they arch slightly upward as shown in the prestressed drawing. Now put the beam back between the books and place weights upon it. You will see that the block beam straightens out and that it will also hold more when stressed below its center.

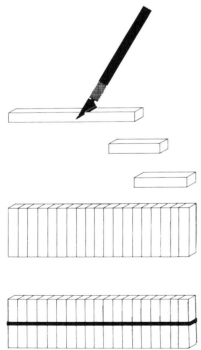

THE SHELL

Shell construction is the same in architecture as it is in nature. A shell is a curvilinear form of rigid material. It can be made very thin in nature. In architecture it must rest upon supports and the shell must be perforated by doors and windows. For this reason shell forms must be altered in building for these special conditions. However, the underlying principles are the same.

A good way to understand the stresses that a shell must withstand is to take an egg in your hand and try to crush it. If the egg is fresh and does not have any cracks you will not be able to break it.

Your hand squeezing the shell is applying tangential forces (parallel) to the shell's curvature. Now take a pencil with a sharp point and tap the shell. It will perforate easily.

The shell can withstand a great deal of pressure along its surface but very little concentrated stress at any one point.

The function of a shell structure in architecture is to transmit forces applied to its surface along its curvature to its supports. If you take one half of an egg shell, place it on a flat surface and push downward, you will find that the shell begins to pull apart at the bottom edge.

It is therefore necessary to have a tension ring or some means of supporting the bottom edge of the shell to keep it from pulling apart.

The shell is infinitely strong, but it must be constructed of materials that can be easily curved. Concrete is probably the best material that we have at the present time for shell construction. But the concrete must be held in place until it sets. Making forms to hold the concrete in place until it hardens can become quite complicated. For this reason one of the most popular shell forms is one called the hyperbolic parabola, a shell curved in two directions that can be formed with straight pieces of wood.

To see how this works make a model.

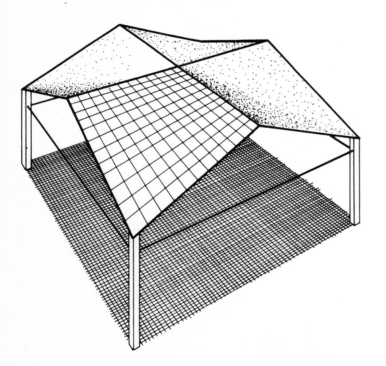

PROJECT 25 — Build a shell of thread.

Materials: Cheap thin cardboard, thread, glue, waxed paper.

Tools: Knife or cutting instrument, needle, pins.

Procedure: Use the waxed paper to protect your working surface which should be soft enough to stick pins into. First cut two strips of cardboard ten inches long and one-half of an inch wide. Measure one-quarter of an inch markings down the center of each piece of cardboard. Place the cardboard pieces ten inches apart exactly oppo-

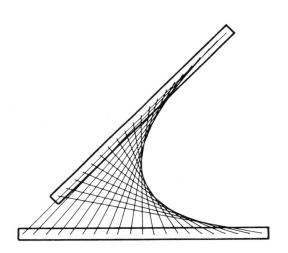

PROJECT 26 — Build a curved shell with straight pieces of cardboard.

Materials: Eight or ten pieces of cheap thin cardboard eight and one-half inches wide by twelve or fourteen inches long. (The backs of pads of notebook paper are ideal.) White glue, waxed paper.

Tools: Cutting tool

Procedure: Cut the cardboard into strips one-quarter of an inch wide and eight and one-half inches long. Cut two cardboard right triangles as shown in the drawing. Glue flanges to one side so that they will stay upright while you are working. Cover the triangles with waxed paper and begin gluing the cardboard strips together as shown.

When the glue has dried, lift off the shell and load it with books to see what happens. It will spread apart where its points rest on the table. What should you do to prevent this from happening?

site and parallel to each other. Put pins in the quarter inch markings. Wind the thread between the pins and put a drop of glue to hold the thread to the cardboard. When the glue dries pull out the pins and remove the model from the waxed paper.

Lift up the two pieces of cardboard holding the thread taut between them. Bend them in opposite directions and look across the thread. You will see a hyperbolic parabola.

You can now make a shell of cardboard.

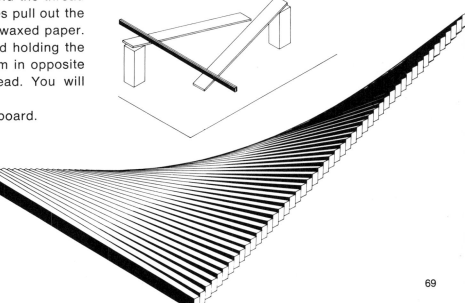

THE FOLDED PLATE

Although the folded plate resembles the ridged roof it is an entirely new type of construction without precedent.

Its principles are easy to understand. It acts like a series of beams on edge butting against each other at the ridges at the top and in the valleys where they meet at the bottom. This structural form can be strong and rigid but it has weaknesses. To find these try this.

Take a sheet of paper and lay it between two books. The paper is not strong enough to support its own weight. Now take the paper and crease it into a series of equal folds. It will now span the books and perhaps support a ruler. If additional weight is applied, however, it will collapse. This can be prevented by gluing a flat piece of paper across the creases at the end as shown in the drawing.

Let us make a folded plate and see how we can restrain it from flattening.

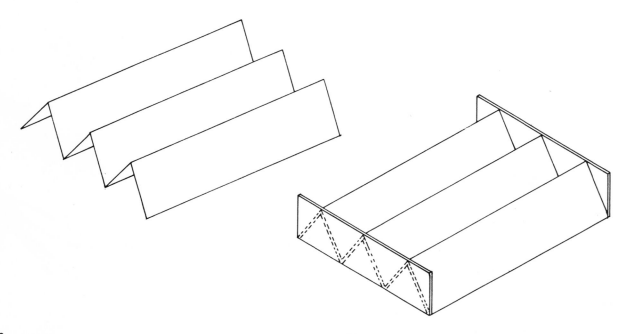

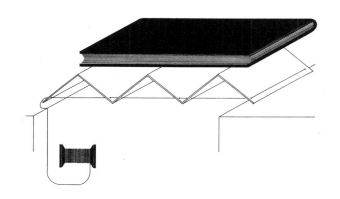

CABLES AND SHELLS

Cable structures are probably the simplest of all structures to understand. The cable is a purely tensile member. When used compressively it falls back on its own weight. For example try to make ten inches of sewing thread stand up straight. However we have found in our model experiments that this same thread can exert considerable strength when used in tension.

Cables are usually combined with compressive members such as the ridge pole of a tent or the towers of suspension bridges. However they have many more possibilities than these traditional uses.

As you will recall earlier in the book in our study of the arch, the tensile catenary form of the cable when reversed became a perfect compressive form for the arch.

Project 27 — Build a folded plate.

Materials: A sheet of light cardboard eighteen inches wide and thirty-two inches long, glue, thread and some scraps of light cardboard.
Tools: Mat knife or cutting instrument.
Procedure: Mark off the cardboard as shown on the drawing, cut lightly along the marks, first on top and then on the bottom. Do not cut all the way through. The cuts are to aid in folding the cardboard.

The objective is to find a means of restraining the folded plate that you have made. It should be supported on its four corners only, do not lay it flat on the table.

The best way to do this is to try different methods of holding the folds together. Observe how it acts under loading and then try to find a way to prevent this action.

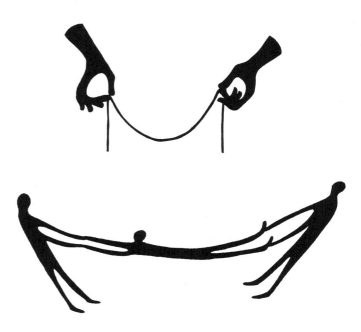

A remarkable application of this principle was employed by Gaudi. He built models for his buildings by suspending weights on wires. By studying the lines of force in these tensile structures Gaudi was able to convert them to the daring compressive masonry forms he used in his buildings.

You can approximate this idea by converting tensile structures to compressive with newspapers, glue, thread and weights. Let us construct a series of shells using Gaudi's idea to learn what we can about converting tension to compression.

PROJECT 28 — Build a hanging shell.

Materials: Flat piece of wood (an old drawing board twenty-four by thirty inches would be fine) or heavy piece of cardboard for mounting, cup hooks, metal washers, spool of #50 thread, newspaper, library paste and basin of water.

Tools: Scissors

Procedure: Screw the cup hooks into the mounting board and tie the thread to them. Use a metal washer to hold the thread down if you wish to make pointed forms. If you want rounded ones the weight of the newspaper will be enough. Wet the newspapers, paint them with paste, tear them into strips and hang them on the threads. Let them take the curvature they will naturally from their weight and the pull of gravity. When the paper and paste dries, cut the threads and turn your newspaper shell right side up.

Make a number of experiments like this. Make as many different curvatures as you can and use several layers of newspaper. When you have built several shells like this test them to see what happens when they are loaded.

With this last project you have completed a series of models beginning with simple masonry (sugar cubes) and progressing through some of the most important ideas of modern architectural structure. These were not all of the ideas of either old or new architecture, but they are some of the most important and most fun to build.

You now know something of building principles, which we have called the architectural alphabet. The next step is to use building principles to form words by expressing our thoughts in building.

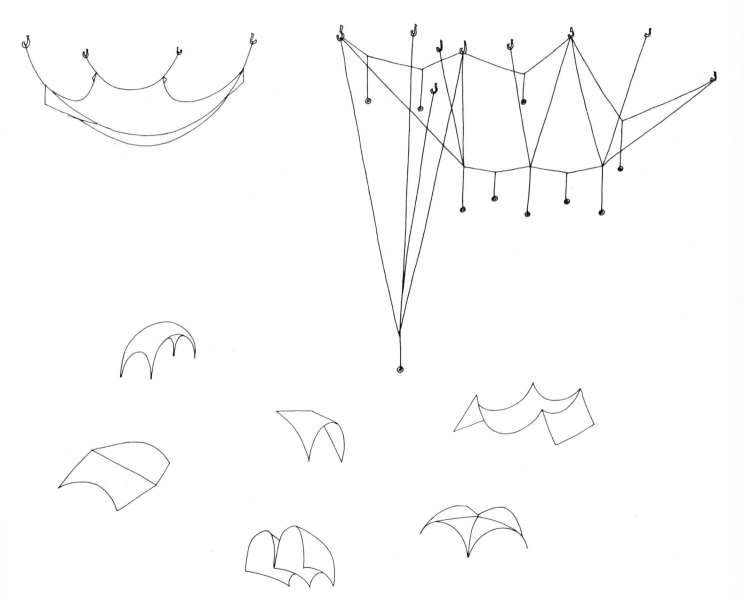

PART 3
THE LANGUAGE OF ARCHITECTURE

In the first two sections of this book we have experimented with the means of building buildings. We will now study how these means can be used to design buildings.

There are aesthetic rules for building just as there are principles of structure. The difference is that if we do not follow structural principles the building will fall down, but if we violate the rules of design the building may continue to stand but will be very ugly. Anyone can tell when a building falls down but not everyone agrees on what makes a building beautiful.

Up to this point we have been able to state the problem and point out solutions. In this last section we will indicate the problem, but the solutions are as many and varied as there are ideas in the reader's head and his ability to express them.

The more you have learned of the alphabet of structure the more architectural words you will be able to design.

SCALE

When we speak of scale in architecture we speak of size, but as with scales that measure quantities by weight, we also speak of balance. The relation of the size of the building to a human being is sometimes called the building's scale. The balance implied in this instance is a gauge of the architect's selection of the size of the building and its elements in relation to each other and to the human beings who will occupy the building. This is a subjective evaluation, an emotional response that is perhaps no more scientifically definable than our enjoyment of music.

However this scale is influenced by a number of intuitive factors. Natural materials are worked into forms in buildings very similar to those they have in nature. For example wood is light and easily worked: it can be bent and fashioned as a structural support in all directions, similar to the branches growing from the trunk of a tree. Stone in building rests in the foundation in the same hard compressive mass that the mountain rests upon the earth. Tunneling in the earth forms a natural arch of which brick construction is a reflection. Instinctively we judge size and scale in terms of these natural forms.

This is another balance of scale which is definable because it has to do with the strength of materials. There are, within certain limits, definable proportions for buildings and building elements which are governed by the laws of engineering. These balances can be calculated and it will be found that in natural materials they will conform remarkably to our instinctive estimation of the materials' capabilities. More sophisticated materials made by man such as tensioned concrete and steel create unfamiliar balances that we must learn.

For example contrast the size of a stone lintel with that of a steel beam required to span the same distance and support the same weight. There is a difference in scale between stone and steel directly related to the strength of the material.

This scale demanded by the strength of materials is as reasonable as the carefully calculated geometric laws of symmetry. But in this case the measuring device is not the column diameter as we discussed at the beginning of the book but the basic unit of the material's fiber stress.

To illustrate this point if you will look at the accompanying drawings you will see a person drawn against a background of differently scaled blocks. If you were asked to draw conclusions about what these background materials were, you would say that the first was stone, the second concrete block and the third brick and the fourth impossible to describe. Why would this be your reaction? Because this is the proportion in which these materials are most commonly encountered. We have seen the human figure against these backgrounds. But there is another idea that we have subconsciously absorbed and that is that these are the natural sizes for the strength of these materials. Stone can be worked in large blocks which would not make much sense in concrete block or brick. In the last drawing we know this material is not structural because its joints are contrary to structural laws as you learned at the beginning of the book with sugar cubes.

The following three projects are concerned with visual effects. They illustrate how patterns of light and shade, or texture, in construction change the appearance of the building.

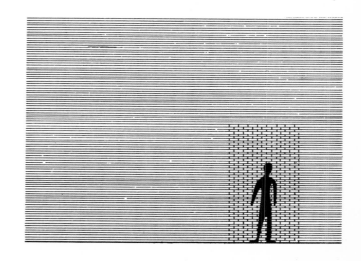

PROJECT 29 — How to change the appearance of a flat circle.

Materials: Drafting paper
Tools: Compass, ruler, pencil
Procedure: Draw a circle and see if by dividing it geometrically you can change its appearance in other ways than those shown in the drawing.

PROJECT 30 — How to change the inside appearance of a cube.

Materials: Light good quality cardboard that can be either inked or painted, triangle, T square, ink, pen, ruler and drafting board or flat surface to work on, white glue.
Tools: Cutting instrument.

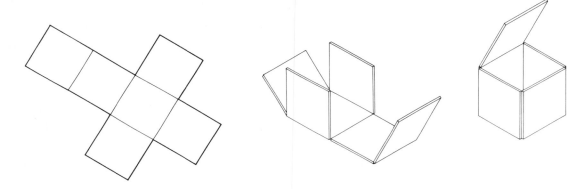

Procedure: Draw the outlines of a cube about six inches square to be made from the cardboard (see drawing). Draw various patterns on the cube surfaces that will form the inside of the cube when it has been cut out and glued together. When you have finished with your design, cut out the cube and glue the edges in place. Place the cardboard figure you used for scale inside the cube to see how the surface designs change the appearance of an interior space in relation to a person.

How would you make the cube appear larger inside, or smaller? How would you make it appear deeper? From these experiments you can see that it is possible to optically change the appearance of a room without changing its size structurally.

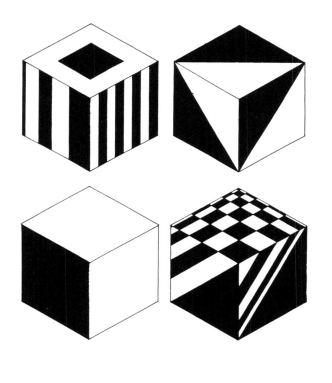

PROJECT 31 — How to change the outside appearance of a cube.

Material: Four pieces of light cardboard with a good quality surface at least twelve inches wide, sixteen inches long. Pen, straight edge, colors if you care to use them, white glue.

Tools: Cutting tool, either single edged razor blade or mat knife.

Procedure: Make four blocks four inches square as shown in the drawing. We will now try to make two of the blocks look larger and two of them look smaller by drawing designs on their surfaces.

In this instance it is probably best to glue the blocks together before marking them. They can be marked first with pencil and later gone over with ink when you have decided on the design that you wish. Try a variety of textures, lines and colors if you have them.

Optical illusions are often part of architecture. For example straight lines will often appear to bow in and out because of curved lines placed next to them as shown in these two drawings. In the laby-

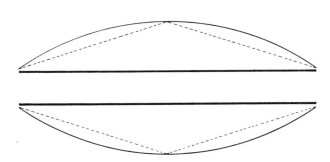

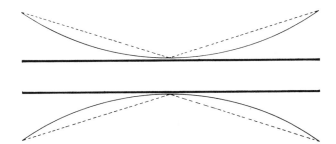

rinth drawing, a white line is surrounded by a black one or is it the other way around? If you look at the drawing for a few minutes the two will appear to be changing places with each other.

TEXTURES

Texture like scale is often intuitively selected by the architect. In childhood, we acquire a knowledge of the world around us by bumping into things, feeling, biting and taking everything apart that comes within our reach.

This knowledge is accumulated and stored in our minds throughout our lifetime. It solidifies into deeply instilled, instinctive opinions about materials. The architect must add to and refine this knowledge because he must use it consciously. For the architect feelings are not enough. He must know as consciously as he can the subconscious effect material will have on others and use this knowledge in the creation of his design.

The following project is set forth to revive some of our feeling for materials and help us to analyze them.

PROJECT 32 — Feeling material.

Material: Any cardboard box or carton at least twelve inches square or a little larger: An assortment of tactile materials, e.g. stone, wood, newspaper, hunks of plaster, smooth glass, sandpaper, anything you can think of.
Tools: Sketch pad and pencil.
Procedure: Cut a hole in the box large enough to put your hand in without seeing into the box. Have a friend put several of the objects in the box without your seeing what they are. When the objects have been placed reach in and feel them. Using your pencil and pad of paper translate graphically what the material feels like.

Try to think of where you would use each material in a building and the kind of feeling that it would give you. Is it strong, is it light, is it fun, soft, etc.?

You can see that it is possible to have a great many feelings about materials that you are not aware of. Now when you use a material in a design you must consider all of the things you thought about it when you did not know what exactly it was but could only feel it.

SPACE

Space is a function of structure although its size is no indication of its architectural value. "People have an instinct about space," said architect Philip Johnson, "but cannot talk about it." Perhaps he is right; however, there are certain effects that space has upon people that seem to be definable. Some people disagree with Mr. Johnson and say that these effects are as definable as engineering proportions.

For instance, we know that space can encourage interpersonal relationships or keep people apart

You can test the instinctive subconscious reaction people have to space by making the following experiment. Anthropologists have discovered that southern Europeans automatically maintain a separation of about twelve inches when conversing and consequently called them a nose to nose culture. Americans are an arm's length culture; they remain about twenty-six inches apart when talking to one another. The next time you find yourself standing to talk with a friend move forward slightly. Without any awareness of the action, in most cases, your friend will move back to establish the standard arm's length separation. You may further test the automatic reactions and subconscious feeling people have about space by watching how

and it may have nothing to do with size. Many people may congregate in the great spaces of a railway station but be kept apart. On the other hand, in the confines of a small room many people will come together at a party. However, the magnitude of the space is not an inducement to communication or an alienation by itself. It is the design of the space that gives it meaning.

We know that animals react strongly to space. If they are not properly provided for spatially they will die. On the other hand, under similar conditions people will adjust. How much this damages them mentally by building up tensions and mental illness from unnatural confinement we do not know. Some psychiatrists have even specified the exact dimensions of the minimal amount of space each person needs in different cultures to maintain his well being.

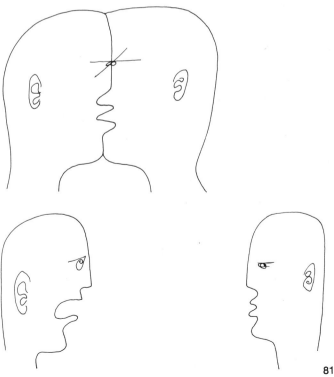

we automatically arrange ourselves in crowds. If there is room they will move into small islands of space, however if we are crowded tightly against each other as in a subway we will try not to notice each other.

When we consider the effects of space, other than in extreme circumstances of either crowding or isolation, we have difficulty in defining its exact influence upon people. We must often use our instincts. Scale and space are components of architecture which are often emotionally evaluated.

We can understand the physical elements that create our various emotional reactions to space and use them in design. For instance, repetition of elements will increase the apparent size of a surface, as we learned in our previous experiments. Rooms with furniture seem much larger than empty ones of the same size. It is possible to produce a sense of depth or height with false perspective. Color may give illusions of largeness or smallness. One dark wall among three light walls in a room seems to increase its size. If you wish to test these ideas further, return to the boxes of the last two projects and try them.

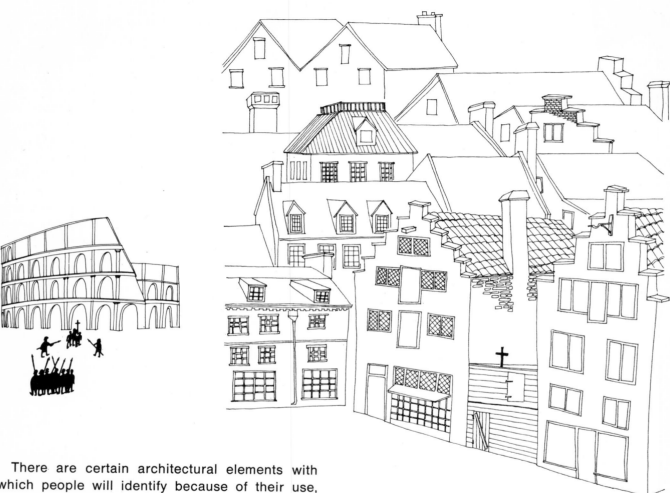

There are certain architectural elements with which people will identify because of their use, such as doors and windows. Furniture, of course, gives us a sense of scale automatically. Westerners always feel much larger than they are in a Japanese room because the furniture is so close to the floor.

We perceive space and distinguish scale by its boundaries, by sound reflection and relative motion, the variability of light and the character of its boundary. There is a completely different spatial experience when driving over a suspension bridge where the cables and the bridge supports are at the side of the roadway than there is when driving over a bridge whose arch is concealed below.

MAN IN SPACE

Thus far we have examined structural systems primarily as structure with secondary interest in the type of space they created. We will now begin from the opposite premise and design from the inside out. We will think of space for its own sake and structure as the generator of the space.

This time we will not choose a structural system for its economy and efficiency but for the emotional meaning of its structure, for the spaces and patterns that it creates. We will be concerned with the effect on our sensibilities of the created space as we move through it.

To do this a specific idea is necessary. We have come to associate form and material partially through habit, but primarily through an innate rightness suggested to us by our sensibilities and we have been educating our sensibilities with our experiments in structure. Now we must be guided by these to create a mood. For instance do not think of the space in terms of a hospital space, a school, a church or an amusement park, but rather in the abstract terms of healing, learning, reverence or fun. In other words, think of the mood you are trying to create, not architectural or graphic forms that identify these kinds of buildings like the pointed arch, a cross or a school bell.

As tools you have the space, solids, and rhythms of architectural elements, textures and color. For example what is a fun place? If you decide that it should provide amusement, the pleasantly unexpected and is constructed for no other purpose than to please, than you might invent a building system that at the exact moment you orient yourself to it, reverses itself in color, form and space.

The form of a church is extremely difficult to create without reverting to stylized religious symbols. To create reverence without the cross, the six pointed star, the pointed arch or the onion dome is a very difficult problem. Schools and hospitals are similarly difficult.

The problem becomes less difficult once you have decided what you want to express. You will then begin to think in terms of all you have learned to express your idea. What kind of structure will best express what you want to say. How will it control light, what does the upward movement of the arch mean contrasted to the downward sag of a cable. Are flat walls or the rhythms of columns best for what you wish to say. These are the decisions the architect makes and those you will make when designing your structure. In reality they are the same that the first builder made when he left the cave and the same man will make on the moon and the planets beyond.

PROJECT 33 — Design a space.

Materials: Any that you choose.
Procedure: It would be preferable to work with the scale that we established in the measurements of the human body. Building to scale assume that the person is about six feet tall and that the structure should cover approximately 200 square feet. The ceiling height and the form of the space are dependent upon your design sense.

Build a building.

APPENDIX

Glossary

A

ARCH. An arrangement of building materials usually in the form of a curve capable of carrying a superimposed load over an opening to its supports.

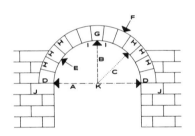

A. Span — the horizontal distance between the springs of the arch.
B. Rise — the vertical distance between the spring line of the arch and the underside of the top stone.
C. Radius — the distance between the arch center (K) and the underside of the top stone.
D. Spring line.
E. Intrados, or soffit, the underside of the arch stones.
F. Extrados, the outside or top of the arch stones.
G. Key stone.
H. Voussoirs (voo'-swars'), the stones of the arch.
I. Crown, the top of the arch.
J. Abutments, The masonry that prevents the arch from sliding horizontally.
K. Arch Center, The point from which the radius begins.

ARCH CENTER. A frame to support the arch while it is being built.
ARCHITECTURE. The art of building.

B

BAY. A compartment or section in the length of a building between each pair or roof trusses of transverse vaulting. A similar compartment of a framed floor between girders. Each space from pillar to pillar.
BEAM. Any horizontal structural member resting upon two or more supports. A mechanism for transferring vertical loads horizontally to the supports.

A.

B.

C.

D.

E.

A. Simple
B. Cantilever
C. Overhanging
D. Continuous
E. Fixed

BOND. Tying the various parts of a masonry wall by lapping one unit over another. Also refers to the pattern formed by the exposed faces of the bricks. The adhesion of the mortar to the bricks is also called a bond.

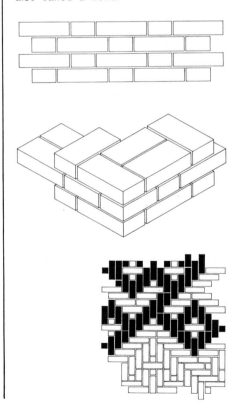

BREAKING JOINTS. The arrangement of masonry units so as to prevent continuous vertical points in adjacent courses.

BUTTRESS. In masonry, a vertical mass projecting from the wall to resist the outward thrusts of vaults, domes, or other forces.

Drawing shows a section through the buttress of a Gothic cathedral. Dotted line represents the wall thickness between buttresses.

C

CANTILEVER. A projecting beam or member supported only at one end.

CATENARY. The form taken by a chain or heavy cord held between two supports. Its form is almost the same as that of a parabola.

CEILING. The covering of a room which hides the roof framing of the floor above.

COLUMN. An upright single member, usually cylindrical in classic architecture, and of a great variety of cross-sectional shapes in modern architecture. Its parts in classic architecture are: the base upon which it rests; its body, called the shaft; and the head, called the capital. The capital may finish with a horizontal slab, called the abacus, and the column's base may rest upon another base called the plinth.

A. Round
B. Square
C. Steel H Column
D. Cruciform
E. Scalloped
F. Clustered columns

CEMENT. In broad terms the word cement refers to any cementitious material that is capable of cementing other materials, usually sand and gravel into an integral mass. Natural cement is made from quarried natural rock. Cement used by the Romans was a combination of slaked lime and volcanic stone. Modern cement or Portland Cement is obtained by mixing and burning two kinds of natural rock and pulverizing the resulting clinkers into a powder. This powder is mixed with water, sand and concrete in carefully specified proportions to produce concrete.

COMPRESSION. Force acting on a body which has the tendency to shorten it.

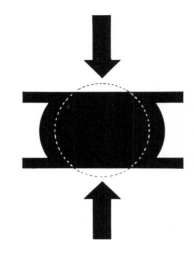

CORBEL. A projection from the face of a wall. In masonry, a succession of such

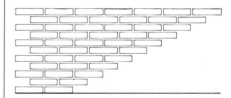

graduated projections may form a corbelled arch.

CORNICE. A projecting horizontal feature, usually molded, which crowns an external facate, or occurs internally at the junction of a wall and a ceiling. In classic architecture, the topmost member of the entablature.

COURSE. One of the continuous horizontal layers of masonry bonded together with mortar and forming the masonry structure.

CURTAIN WALL. A thin wall between structural members that is non-load-bearing.

D

DEFLECTION. The bending of a structural member under pressure.

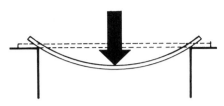

DEFORMATION. A force acting upon a body causing an accompanying change in the shape and size of the body.

DOME. A convex roof of approximately hemispherical form erected over a square octagonal or circular space in a building. Cupola is an almost synonymous term.

E

EQUILIBRIUM. When a system of forces is in equilibrium they equal (or balance) each other, preventing movement. Downward forces equal upward; horizontal to the right equal horizontal to the left.

ENTABLATURE. In classical architecture the arrangement of the horizontal members above the supporting columns. This lintel was divided into three parts named the architrave, frieze and cornice. Together they became the entablature.

F

FACADE. The face or front of a building.

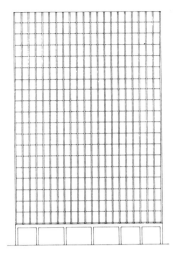

FLYING BUTTRESS. A detached buttress at some distance from a wall and connected to it by an arch or portion of an arch so as to thrust against the wall.

FORCE. That which exerts motion, pressure, or tension on a body, either tending to move it or change its shape. In building construction we are only concerned with statics, which is the study of bodies at rest under the action of forces.

FOUNDATION WALL. That portion of a load-bearing wall below the level of the adjacent grade or below the first floor beams.

FRAMING. In wood construction, the rough timber work of the house, including the flooring, roofing, partitioning, ceiling and beams. In steel construction, the columns, beams and girders. Usually refers to the skeleton of the building.

G

GIRDER. A large beam used to support joists or walls over an opening.

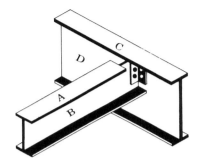

A. Flange of beam
B. Web of beam
C. Web of girder
D. Flange of girder

GOLDEN SECTION. A geometrical law which for centuries has been regarded as the key to harmonic proportions. The usual formula is to cut a finite line so that the shorter part is to the longer as the longer is to the whole.

H

HEADER. In masonry, the short end of a brick or stone. (The stretcher is the long side of the brick.) In carpentry, the large beam into which the common joists are framed.

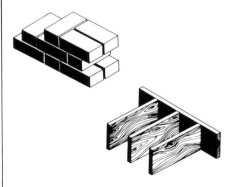

HYPERBOLIC PARABOLOID. A complex parabolic surface resembling a saddle that can be formed by a straight line with its two ends on straight lines askew in space.

J

JOINERY. Light woodwork of a building (e.g. frames around doors and windows) as distinguished from carpentry. The finished woodwork as distinguished from the structural framing.

JOINT. The uniting of two materials. The connection of like materials where their surface is not continuous.

JOIST. Light beams upon which the floor is supported.

L

LATERAL SUPPORT. Support from the sides.

LINTEL. A horizontal member of wood, stone, or steel across the top of a door or window opening to carry the load of the building above it.

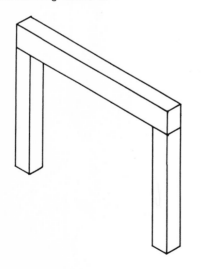

M

MASONRY. Brick, tile, stone or other similar building units or combinations bonded together with mortar.

MEMBER. A unit of the whole. A joist or a rafter is a structural member. The joist is part of the floor framing and the rafter part of the roof framing.

MODULE. This word was used in historic architecture for determining the proportions of various parts of a columnar system. The column diameter being taken as a unit of measure. In modern architecture the module is a convenient unit upon which all dimensions of a building and its components are based. The term may also be used as a unit of measure applying to building elements. Such as the related module or size of bricks.

MORTAR. A plastic mixture of cementitious materials used to bond bricks or other types of masonry units together.

MOLDINGS. Ornamental and continuous lines or grooving or projections.

MOMENT. A moment is force times distance. It has a tendency to cause rotation around a certain point. The magnitude of the moment is its force times its distance from a given point.

MULLION. In Medieval and Renaissance architecture, a vertical member of wood or stone dividing the sections of a window. In modern architecture, the vertical member dividing windows.

O

OCTAGON. A figure having eight wides.

P

PENDENTIVE. In the construction of a dome resting upon a square base, the spherical triangle formed between each pair of supporting arches.

PIER. The solid parts of a wall between windows and voids. The solid part of walls where they are increased in thickness to carry heavier loads such as lintels, beams, girders, or trusses.

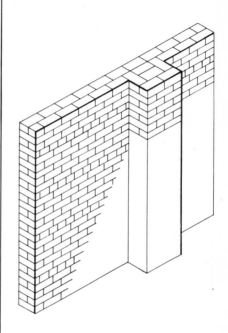

PINACLE. An ornament forming the crown of a buttress. It was used as a weight to counteract the thrust of other parts of the construction. On top of a flying buttress it helps the buttress counteract the push of the vaults.

PLAN. A drawing of the various parts of any floor or story of a building projected upon a horizontal plane.

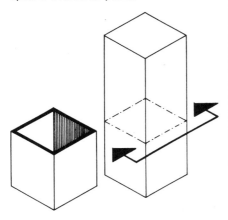

PLASTER. There are two kinds of plaster, lime and gypsum. Lime plaster is made from limestone and gypsum plaster from gypsum rock. Both stones are burned, purified and ground to a powder. When water is added they harden back into a stone like mass.

POST. A piece of timber erected in a vertical position to support some part of the structure of a building.

R

RAFTER. A roof joist.

REVEAL. The side of a doorway or window opening that is not covered by the door or window frame. That part of the opening that is revealed.

S

SECTION. A drawing showing the internal heights of the various parts of a building. It supposes the building to be cut through vertically, so as to exhibit the walls, the heights of the internal doors and other apertures, the heights of the stories, thicknesses of floors, etc.

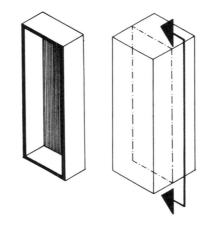

SHEAR. The resistance of a body to being cut by the action of two parallel forces or loads acting in opposite directions.

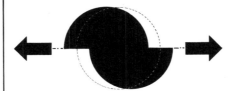

SKIN. The exterior surface of a building which is not load-bearing. A term used in place of curtain wall.

SOFFIT. The underside of a lintel, arch or cornice.

SPANDREL OR SPANDRIL. The space between an arch or curved brace and the beams over the same. In skeleton construction, an exterior wall between columns or piers and wholly supported at each story. The spandrel beam supports the spandrel wall.

SQUINCH OR SQUINCH ARCH. A small arch built obliquely across each internal angle of a square tower or other structure in order to carry a circular dome or octagonal spire.

STATICS. The branch of mechanics which treats the equilibrium of forces, or relates to bodies held in equilibrium by forces acting on them.

STRESS. An internal resistance to an external force. A direct stress is when the entire cross-sectional area of the member is stressed uniformly.

STRUCTURE. The load-bearing members of a building such as the columns, beams, and girders.

T

TENSION. When a force acts upon a body in such a manner that the body tends to lengthen or pull apart.

THRUST. The downward and outward pressure or force exerted by a dome, vault or arch or other structural member upon its supporting walls or piers.

TRUSS. A framed structural member, usually triangulated, designed to bear superimposed loads. The truss is designed so that its members will support loads in compression or tension rather than resisting bending forces.

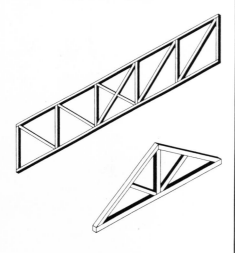

V

VAULT. An arched ceiling or roof.

Bibliography

The reader will, I hope, excuse the frank prejudices expressed in describing the following books. Many of them have been my friends and references for a period of years. Much that I have written in this book has been influenced by the ideas and thinking of these authors. Exactly how much came from each I have no way of knowing since we tend to digest and assimilate ideas we like and usurp them for our own. It is for this reason I did not attempt to give individual references throughout the text.

The appropriation of ideas in structure (unlike architecture, which bears the signature of the individual architect) has been going on for centuries. Ideas in building are to be adopted, added to, and passed on. They are not things that men sign their names to. None of these authors invented architecture or building. What they did was to give fresh insights and inspire others to make their contribution to the art of building.

Ambrose, James E. *Building Structures Primer.* New York: John Wiley & Sons, Inc., 1967.
Structure without mathematics from an architectural viewpoint. The format is that of an expanded encyclopedia. Excellent photographs and drawings. The book describes not only structure but structural systems, materials, and analysis.

Le Corbusier. *The Modulor.* Cambridge: Harvard University Press, 1954.
An account of the invention of the author's modulor system and its use. A bit mystical but worthwhile.

Cowan, Henry J. *An Historical Outline of Architectural Science.* New York: Elsevier Publishing Company, 1966.
A very short history of architectural science. It will most benefit the student who has gained a little knowledge. The author describes environmental design (climate control in buildings through mechanical systems) lighting, systems building and materials. It will give the reader a broader picture of the history and the contemporary condition of building science than those books dealing with structure alone.

Fitch, James Marston. *American Building, The Historical Forces that Shaped It.* Boston: Houghton Mifflin Company, The Riverside Press, Cambridge, 1966.
The classic book on the architecture of the United States. The author, one of the most knowledgeable scholars in the field, writes very well, with significant historical references and penetrating social comment.

Fletcher, Sir Banister. *A History of Architecture on the Comparative Method.* New York City: Charles Scribner's Sons, 1963. (Seventeenth edition.)
The encyclopedia of ancient and historic European architecture. Styles and building methods are compared and analyzed against their historic backgrounds. Many photographs, well-executed drawings, plans, sections and details. Modern architecture of the East are briefly described. An essential book for the serious student.

Giedion, Sigfried. *Space, Time and Architecture.* Cambridge: Harvard University Press, 1952.
A well-known book, extremely important for its author's ideas. His self-expressed purpose: "My interest has been particularly concentrated on the growth of the new tradition in architecture, for the purpose of showing its interrelations with other human activities and the similarity of methods that are in use today in architecture, construction, painting, city planning and science."

Hamlin, Talbot. *Architecture Through The Ages.* New York: G. P. Putnam's Sons, 1940.
A history of architecture, very pleasantly written. The structural descriptions are imaginative and first rate. Probably still one of the best books for the student to begin his study of the history of architecture.

Kouwenhoven, John A. *The Arts in Modern American Civilization* (Originally published under the title *Made in America*). New York: W. W. Norton and Company, Inc., 1967. (Paperback)
Although the author describes all the arts, his description of architecture is particularly good. For an understanding of the forces that have created the architecture of the United States this book should also be required reading for every design sudent.

Murray, Peter. *Architecture of the Italian Renaissance.* New York: Schocken Books Inc., 1966 (Paperback.)
A very fine account of the architecture of this period. Numerous photographs and drawings.

Parker, Harry. *Simplified Engineering for Architects and Builders.* New York: John Wiley & Sons, Inc., 1961.
For the more serious student this book is invaluable. It describes simple structural theory and equips the student to handle small structures. The mathematics involved are not above the level of high school algebra.

Pevsner, Nickolaus. *An Outline of European Architecture.* Baltimore, Maryland: Pelican Books, Inc., 1963. (Paperback.)
Pevsner's book is thought by some, myself among them, to be the best short history of European architecture ever published. Best or not, it is close to it, with a lively fresh approach by one of the great architectural historians of our day.

Rasmussen, Steen Eiler. *Experiencing Architecture.* Cambridge: M.I.T. Press, 1964. (Paperback.)
Rasmussen conveys everything architecture is: color, rhythm, texture, light and sound. You will never again look at a building without truly seeing if after reading this book. For the sheer joy of architecture this book is the best.

Rudofsky, Bernard. *Architecture Without Architects.* Garden City, New York: The Museum of Modern Art distributed by Doubleday and Co., Inc., 1964.
A fascinating book mostly photographs with descriptions of buildings seldom seen in the pages of architectural histories.

Salvadori, Mario and Robert Heller. *Structure in Architecture.* Englewood Cliffs, New Jersey: Prentice-Hall, Inc., 1963.
A comprehensive, simply explained study of structure with clearly presented drawings, without mathematics.

Vitruvius, translated by Morris Hicky Morgan. *The Ten Books of Architecture.* New York: Dover Publications, 1960. (Paperback.)
A description of classic architecture by the famous first century A.D. Roman architect. Fine as history, also contains excellent descriptions of Roman building techniques. Perhaps not the best translation, but absorbing reading and a good reference book for your library. (Incidentally, Dover Publications manages to publish numerous architectural and related books at reasonable prices. They also published Palladio's *Four Books or Architecture,* a perfect companion to Vitruvius.)

Wachsman, Konrad. *The Turning Point of Building.* New York: Reinhold Publishing Corporation, 1961.
A classic on the industrialization of building. Superlative photographs and drawings present the philosophy of this very important architect and thinker.

Wilson, Forrest. *What it Feels Like to be a Building.* Doubleday, 1968.
A book for very young readers by myself and a very good editor. This book is mostly drawings which translate building and structural principles into physical feelings.

Zuk, William. *Concepts of Structure.* New York City: Reinhold Publishing Corporation, 1963.
A concise description of structural principles. Simply explained, well-written, excellent diagrams.

MANUFACTURER'S PAMPHLETS

The various large corporations and institutes such as Bethlehem Steel, the Concrete Institute, Anaconda Copper and others publish booklets which are helpful to the student. They are usually written for the practicing architect, and although some of the technical information may be beyond the understanding of the beginning student, they are helpful and informative. These books describe the latest techniques and picture their building application.

One of their appealing features is that they are often given free to students. Write to the Press or Public Relations Departments of individual companies to obtain them.